The *Parents*™ Magazine Baby and Child-Care Series combines the most up-to-date medical findings, the advice of doctors and child psychologists, and the actual day-to-day experiences of parents like you. Covering a wide variety of subjects, these books answer all your questions, step-by-important-step, and provide the confidence of knowing you're doing the best for your child—with help from *Parents*™ Magazine.

"A sensitive, realistic discussion of allergic conditions in children and how parents can help them be as healthy, active, and happy as possible."

> from the foreword by
> Warren Richards, M.D.
> Head, Division of Allergy-Clinical Immunology;
> Director, Ambulatory Services,
> Childrens Hospital of Los Angeles;
> Professor of Clinical Pediatrics,
> University of Southern California
> School of Medicine

Other PARENTS™ BOOKS
Published by Ballantine Books:

PARENTS™ BOOK OF TOILET TEACHING
PARENTS™ BOOK FOR YOUR BABY'S FIRST YEAR

Parents™
Book of
Childhood Allergies

RICHARD F. GRABER

BALLANTINE BOOKS • NEW YORK

For Ethel
with love and
gesundheit!

Library of Congress Catalog Card Number: 83-90027

ISBN 0-345-30443-8

Manufactured in the United States of America

First Edition: September 1983

Contents

Foreword

If you're the parent of an allergic child, you've probably experienced some frustration in trying to learn about your child's condition. There is no shortage of advice from well-meaning friends and relatives, and bookstore shelves are crammed with titles advocating miracle "cures" for all kinds of allergies. Some of this information may be helpful, but much of it is confusing at best and misleading or incorrect at worst. How can you be sure that you're getting reliable, up-to-date information about your child's allergies?

Parents™ *Book of Childhood Allergies* will be a great help. It authoritatively explodes the myths and the mystery surrounding allergies. The mechanism of allergy and the options for treatment are discussed in a level-headed, clear fashion, with the welfare of the allergic child always at the forefront. Controversial issues in diagnosis and management are explored and put in perspective. If a common recommendation is scientifically correct but just not workable in the day-to-day lives of most allergic children and their families, this problem is pointed out—and a realistic compromise is suggested.

So many children have allergies that significantly affect their lives. They may miss a great deal of school, they often cannot play with their friends, they are embarrassed about their appearance, they can have life-threatening symptoms. Frequently their parents do not realize how much they can contribute to their allergic child's well-being. They need practical answers to basic questions:

"Why?"

"What can be done?"

"How can I help?"

This book provides many of the answers. It is a sensitive, realistic discussion of allergic conditions in children, and how parents can help them be as healthy, active, and happy as possible.

WARREN RICHARDS, M.D.
Head, Division of Allergy-Clinical Immunology,
Children's Hospital of Los Angeles
Professor of Clinical Pediatrics,
University of Southern California School of Medicine

Introduction

It's been estimated that half of the people in the world have an allergy. Whatever the accuracy of that generalization, allergy *is* a major problem in the United States. And because most allergies begin in childhood, it's especially a problem for children, and for their parents.

"Allergy" is not a neat, well-defined disease. It is an umbrella term that covers such diverse conditions and complications as hay fever (nasal allergy), eczema, hives, conjunctivitis (sore, itchy eyes), asthma, gastrointestinal allergy, shock, and more.

Fortunately, children's allergies are usually mild or moderate rather than severe. Some children have allergic reactions so mild that they seldom if ever need medical help. In fact, one very legitimate kind of treatment your doctor can prescribe is no treatment at all, as we discuss later. The best treatment always is the least treatment that will allow your child, no matter what his allergy, to lead an active and happy life.

Allergy is democratic. It doesn't discriminate because of race, sex, income, education, living environment, or any other variable except age (it first shows up much more often in young children than in adults). It is probably the most widespread chronic condition in the country.

According to the best estimates, including recent reports from an allergy and asthma task force of the National Institute of Allergy and Infectious Diseases, more than 35 million people in the United States have allergies (or one out of six). Nearly everyone either has an allergy or knows someone who does.

In children only, reports the task force, 2 to 3 million have allergic bronchial asthma, more than 6 million have nasal allergy (including hay fever), and 2 million have eczema, hives, and other skin and food allergies. Well over 6 million children in the United States have at least one allergy and many have more than one.

While these figures are only estimates, it's useful to realize that many millions of Americans have allergies. If your child is allergic, he has plenty of company. Hundreds of thousands of parents are experiencing the same frustrations, the same demands that you and your spouse may be facing.

Management of allergy in children is improving. Research work in allergy laboratories is providing better understanding of this disease. Today, compared with even ten to twenty years ago, allergists and other physicians know more about the basic mechanism of an allergic reaction than ever before. Better diagnostic

measures are becoming available, and more effica-
cious medicines and other therapies are being intro-
duced. The outlook is optimistic.

Yet much work remains to be done. And rather
than sit around waiting for panaceas from the nation's
laboratories, we need to manage childhood allergies
with simple, preventive measures and with careful attention to the child's physical and emotional needs.
Because it is a chronic condition that is not well understood by the general public, and still regarded as a
psychosomatic illness by many ill-informed people,
allergy demands parental knowledge and support. You
have a great opportunity to be a supportive, positive
influence on your child's life.

This book addresses that opportunity: to explain the
best of the new recommendations as well as the time-
tested practical measures that can help you help your
child. For you, all the recommendations, all the data
in the world come down to what you're able to do for
one individual—your allergic child.

1. What Is Allergy?

Allergy is an abnormal immune response to substances that do not create such a response in a healthy person. The substances can be things we inhale or eat or drink; venom from insect stings; medications, including shots; things we touch and absorb.

There are two basic types of allergy—inherited and acquired. The inherited allergies (actually inherited tendencies, as explained below) include nasal allergy, eczema, asthma, and hives. Most of these allergies occur in children (or adults) with allergic tendencies. The acquired allergies include contact skin allergies, penicillin allergy, and poison ivy, and can occur in any child or adult on exposure, not just those with inherited allergic tendencies. Since inherited allergies are overwhelmingly the most common type in children, that's the kind we talk about in this book. When

we do discuss an acquired allergy, it will be identified
as such.

All of the many inherited allergies share these char-
acteristics:

• Allergic children do not inherit a specific allergy
(such as hay fever) but a tendency to be allergic. If
your child inherits the tendency, she is, by definition,
allergic, even if the tendency is never expressed by
an allergic reaction.

• If a child is allergic, the allergy won't produce
symptoms (you won't even know it's there, in most
cases) until he has been exposed and reexposed to the
substances he's allergic to. We're literally surrounded
by potential allergens (the medical term for the symp-
tom-producing substances), so exposure presumably
begins at an early age, but the reaction may not show
up for days, months, even years—if *ever*.

• Allergens are not toxic in themselves. Children
who are *not* allergic can inhale the pollen or eat the
eggs or pet the cat—whatever sets off an allergic
reaction in your child—and suffer no ill effects. Why
your child and not others? Allergists don't know the
complete answer yet, but mounting evidence points to
genetics as the key, rather than any environmental
factors.

• Classic allergic reactions are *not* infectious, even
though the symptoms may look that way. Allergies
occur only when specific allergens invade a child who
is allergic to them. Other children can't "catch" the
allergy or the symptoms from her.

• Allergies in children sometimes clear up sponta-
neously, but they may remain the same or get worse.
Predicting the outcome is a guess in most cases, be-

cause what causes a certain outcome is not yet understood completely. Early recognition and treatment do help, however, and any child whose allergic symptoms begin to interfere with his daily living should be seen by a physician. If you are not sure your child's problems are caused by an allergic reaction, take him to your doctor anyway. In the early stages of what may be an allergy, err on the conservative side.

• The goal of allergy diagnosis and treatment is to alleviate as much of the patient's discomfort as possible without adding to her burdens by imposing an overly strict regimen. Put another way, the goal is to support happy, functioning children, not to reverse completely every little symptom. You don't want to overwhelm the child with treatment and convert her into a full-time, chronic "patient."

How the Allergic Reaction Works

What happens during an allergic response is a reaction between an antigen and an antibody. An *antigen* is a substance foreign to the body that the body recognizes as foreign. Bacteria that cause infectious diseases in humans and are not part of the normal bacteria in the body are antigens.

An *antibody* is a kind of protein called an immunoglobulin that is one of your body's important defenses. Your body manufactures many different types of antibodies, each designed to combat a specific type of antigen. If you have a cold, for example, the antigen invading your body is a virus, and some of your antibodies are programmed to subdue the virus in an antigen-antibody reaction and return you to good health.

An antigen that results in an allergic reaction is called an *allergen*. Unlike common bacterial and viral antigens, the allergen is not toxic in nonallergic people. But in allergic people, the body develops a response to this normally harmless substance, such as pollen or house dust, after repeated exposures. Why this happens in a person's immune system (the body's defense system) is still not fully understood.

What *is* understood is that the antibody involved is an immunoglobulin called immunoglobulin E (IgE) that is programmed to react with a specific allergen and no others. The IgE antibodies gather on the surface of certain cells, called "mast cells," found primarily in the lining of the nose, throat, lungs, digestive tract, and skin. When an allergen comes in contact with the IgE antibody produced to fight it, several chemicals are released into the surrounding tissue, including histamine. In effect, the immune system *overreacts*. If this reaction takes place in the nose, the histamine dilates blood vessels in the nose and makes the vessel walls more porous; normal tissue fluid leaks into and through the nasal tissue in abnormally large quantities, starting the nasal allergy symptoms of swelling, itching, runny nose, and so on. If the reaction takes place in the lungs or bronchi, it starts the symptoms associated with asthma. If the reaction is primarily in the skin, eczema or hives may result.

It's certainly not necessary for you to understand the physiology of an allergic reaction in order to provide your child with the best care. This understanding is perhaps of more interest to allergists and allergy researchers, and it's comparatively new. It was not until 1967 that IgE, called "the allergy protein," was discovered. If you *are* interested in this unfolding explanation, see Appendix A, "The Allergic Reaction," or consult some of the "Sources of Further Information."

The Parents' Legacy

Children do not inherit allergies; they inherit *a tendency to be allergic*. You'll hear this often from today's allergists.

If both you and your spouse are allergic, your child has a 60 to 75 percent risk of inheriting an allergic tendency. (Some allergists put it another way—that two out of three of your children probably will inherit an allergic tendency.) If you are allergic and your spouse is not, or the reverse, your child has a 25 to 50 percent chance, and if neither you nor your spouse is allergic, he still has a 10 percent chance. Thus even among so-called normal parents, one out of ten children will be allergic, which probably means that all family trees have their allergic branches if you go back a generation or two. (Allergists rightly bristle at the "normal" versus "abnormal" distinction, by the way. Asthmatic children are not abnormal, they point out. They're normal children who happen to have an allergy.)

Your child will not necessarily inherit the same specific allergies that you have. Although he *may* wind up with the same ones, he may just as easily wind up with a different reaction. You may sneeze through every ragwood pollen season, your spouse may wheeze periodically with asthma, and your child may get by with a rash after eating eggs or with watery eyes when he pets the cat.

Some parents whose child is allergic feel responsible for having "given" the child her allergies. They tend to wallow in guilt and often overprotect her while they dwell on their legacy. Such feelings may be understandable, but they do far more harm than good. This kind of guilt serves no purpose. After all, we can't change or direct our genes. And children are quick to sense such guilt feelings and take advantage of them; some become extremely skillful at manipulating their guilt-ridden parents.

Set aside the guilt trip and you can avoid becoming an "allergic parent." Allergists are well acquainted with them. They appear frazzled and worn out. They turn up with hour-by-hour accounts of their child's progress. They concentrate on little but their allergic child.

"I really can't understand how some of these parents keep going," one allergist says. "They seem to devote all of their time to observing and recording their child's allergic reactions. I remind parents that their child is not a case of allergy. Their child is a normal, healthy child who has some allergies. There's a vast difference. Treating your child as a child and not a medical case is the single most important gift a parent can give."

When children know that their parents regard their allergies as a manageable annoyance, and *not* as the central problem of the whole family's existence, they will be less likely to strike back in frustration, and they will be more inventive and active in handling their own symptoms and problems. Some overprotective, oversolicitous parents, once they learn to treat their child as a child, are amazed and delighted at his ability to cope and get along in the world.

A few parents swing to the opposite extreme. They somehow ignore the allergy altogether, which may be hard for you to imagine. They may bring a child into the doctor's office for some reason not related to asthma. The doctor immediately sees that the child is panting and wheezing, very uncomfortable, and nearly exhausted. He assumes the apparent asthma is what brings parent and child in, only to be told, "Oh, that's nothing, doctor. She's been like that all her life."

You shouldn't become a slave to your child's allergies, but you can't ignore them either. Neither extreme helps the child.

Common Reactions and Symptoms

In children, some of the common allergic reactions and complications are:

- Nasal allergy
  —seasonal ("hay fever" or "rose fever")
  —perennial (chronic, year-round pattern)
- Serous otitis media (accumulation of fluid in the middle ear)
- Allergic asthma
- Gastrointestinal disorders from food allergies
- Eczema (atopic dermatitis)
- Hives
- Contact dermatitis (poison ivy rash a prime example)
- Conjunctivitis (eye irritation)
- Anaphylactic reaction (uncommon, serious shock reaction to any allergen)

These are just a few of the most common reactions. A list of symptoms can go on at length too, but here are the more common symptoms, grouped by the reaction that usually causes them:

Nasal allergy symptoms: Nasal congestion; sneezing, especially a series of sneezes in the morning; runny nose; itchy throat and nose; conjunctivitis with puffy lids.

Serous otitis media symptoms: Serous otitis media is an inflammation of the inner ear from fluid buildup that frequently coincides with nasal allergy. Otitis can be present without the child being aware of it. He may reveal temporary hearing loss only by turning the TV or radio excessively loud or missing conversation. Sometimes patients experience a sense of fullness in the ear or pain behind the ear drum.

Eczema symptoms: Intense itching and redness of the skin; a dry, scaly rash appearing only on scratching; later, "weeping" of fluid from the rash. In infants, eczema usually appears on cheeks, forehead, arms, and legs. In older children, it often appears on folds of the knees, elbows, ankles, wrists.

Asthma symptoms: Wheezing; dry coughing; tightness of chest and shortness of breath, especially on exertion. Intermittent attacks often brought on by sustained exercise and exhaustion, some airborne allergens, the strain of having a common cold, emotional reactions, and other "triggers."

Food allergy symptoms: In some patients, gastrointestinal problems such as nausea, vomiting, abdominal pain, diarrhea, constipation, indigestion, colic. In other patients, any of the symptoms for nasal allergy or asthma.

Hives symptoms: Pale, itchy welts surrounded by redness, sometimes similar in appearance to large mosquito bites. Can be accompanied by angioedema, a giant, very serious swelling of deeper tissues.

Contact dermatitis symptoms: Very itchy red pimples or blisterlike eruptions on skin where the allergen touched—e.g., hands and face from poison ivy; wrist from allergy to bracelet. Eruptions, though intensely itchy, not spread by scratching (except in the case of fresh poison ivy, sumac, or oak) but only by further contact.

Conjunctivitis symptoms: Itching eyes; redness of conjunctiva (outer membrane of eye and inner membrane of eyelid); tearing; swollen eyelids.

Anaphylactic reaction symptoms: In mild reactions, common allergic symptoms. In severe reactions, accentuated wheezing and breathing difficulty; shock (falling blood pressure); possible unconsciousness. (See chapter 7, "Allergic Emergencies.")

General symptoms (primarily with nasal allergy and asthma): "Allergic shiner" (dark crescent under eyes from sleeplessness, exhaustion, and pooling of tissue fluids); general malaise; colic in infants; excessive fatigue; change in personality toward irritability and depression; poor skin color and all-around appearance. Symptoms are sometimes linked to seasons or the appearance of allergens or irritants, but other times are capricious.

Many, if not all, of these symptoms can also be caused by other diseases, such as colds, influenza, some skin infections, and throat infections. One of the goals of allergy diagnosis, as your doctor will point out, is to be sure it's really allergies that are causing the problem.

The listing of common allergy symptoms above does look formidable, and a complete list of every symptom that can be involved would look overwhelming. But your child won't have all the symptoms; no child will. Your child may have several symptoms that are common to her allergic condition, but even then her symptoms are far more likely to be mild or moderate than severe.

Common Allergens and Irritants

Again, this list could go on forever, but it's confined to the common allergens and irritants. And there's a distinct difference between the two.

An allergen is a substance that, even in small amounts, can directly cause an allergic reaction if someone is allergic to it. An irritant is *not* capable of causing a specific allergic reaction, but can trigger an allergic condition that already exists.

For example, house dust and certain plant pollens are allergens that cause reactions only in allergic individuals. Tobacco smoke and common cold germs are irritants; they are irritating to many people who are not allergic, and can trigger allergic reactions in people who are.

Common allergens are:

Airborne. Certain weeds, grasses, tree pollens; mold spores; animal dander (bits of skin shed by nearly all animals that don't swim or crawl); house dust (contains insect dust, bits of feathers, bits of fibers from fabrics, bits of kapok, often animal dander, and microscopic mites).

Foods. Common ones affecting allergic children include fish, milk, nuts, berries, shellfish, eggs, chocolate, corn, pork, peas and beans, wheat, and some fruits.

Contact allergens. Poison ivy and related plants; ragweed resin (not the pollen); nickel, chrome, and mercury used in jewelry and watches.

Insect stings. Some sting, some bite. Common insect allergens are venoms from the honeybee, wasp, hornet, yellow jacket, and fire ant.

Drugs (medications). "Drugs" means anything used to treat disease, including vitamins, hormones, serums, and various chemicals. While nearly any drug can be at fault, the more common ones include penicillin; sulfa drugs; thiouracil (used for thyroid or heart conditions); phenytoin (used to treat epilepsy); nitrofurantoin (used to treat urinary tract infection); and sulfasalazine (used to treat intestinal inflammation). Drugs that may cause allergylike symptoms but apparently not true allergic reactions are aspirin; tartrazine (yellow food dye No. 5); dyes used in some X-ray contrast studies; and ampicillin, a commonly prescribed semisynthetic antibiotic.

2. Myths and Misunderstandings

Allergies probably are as old as mankind, but scientific understanding of the allergic reaction and what can be done about it is quite recent. As mentioned, IgE, the "allergy protein," was just discovered in 1967, so it's small wonder that myths, misunderstandings, and controversial treatments are still common.

At times it seems that everyone you talk to—particularly oversolicitous relatives—has a special explanation of allergy and a surefire cure. See how many of the following you're familiar with.

There's no need to treat allergies in children because they outgrow them anyway.

Wrong. Some childhood allergies get better on their own, but you certainly can't count on it. In moderate to severe cases, doing nothing can leave your child chronically ill, probably unnecessarily. Early detection and treatment to prevent or postpone complications are important.

An allergist can tell you whether your child will outgrow the allergy.

Not so. Allergists know only too well that the only prediction they can make with 100 percent accuracy is that the condition will get worse, stay the same, or get better. Because the outcome cannot be predicted, allergies in your child are not something you should try to manage alone. You need your doctor's guidance.

Allergy shots are the only true cure in children.

No. Complete removal of the allergens so your child has no contact with them is the only true cure. Obviously that's possible only in theory, although you can often partially eliminate some of the allergens in her surroundings. Allergy shots (immunotherapy) may help many children live more comfortably with their allergies and are often needed when the allergy is severe.

A child who is allergic to dogs will not be bothered by a short-haired dog as a pet.

False. Allergic reactions from dogs and other animals are caused by dander—small scales from the animal's skin—and not by animal hair. The length of the hair makes no difference.

House plants aggravate allergies in children and should be removed.

Although many patients and physicians believed this for years, recent studies conclusively demonstrate that it is not true. House plants have *not* been shown to aggravate allergic conditions.

Summer-long colds in youngsters are a common part of growing up.

Not so. It's common for children, especially pre-schoolers, to have six to eight colds a year, but the colds generally clear up in a week if there are no complications. A child with a cold that persists for weeks or all summer certainly should be seen by a doctor. He may have an allergy or sinusitis.

Removal of tonsils and adenoids often cures nasal allergy or asthma in children.

No. While there are reasons for removal of tonsils and adenoids in a child, such as recurrent tonsil infection or adenoidal blockage, allergy is not one of them. They should *not* be removed in an effort to alleviate an allergy.

Hay fever (seasonal nasal allergy) happens in the latter part of August and most of September.

Not necessarily. It happens then only if the condition is caused by Eastern ragweed pollen (which *does* account for perhaps 75 percent of cases in the Midwest and East) because this pollen is airborne at that time of year. Other allergens, such as tree and grass pollens and Western ragweed, can cause the reaction at other times and for a longer duration.

Hay fever is caused by exposure to hay in the late summer.

No. Hay fever (seasonal nasal allergy) is not caused by hay but by pollens from weeds, grasses, and trees at different times of the year in different parts of the country.

"Rose fever" is caused by exposure to roses in the late spring.

No. Rose fever (seasonal nasal allergy) is another name for hay fever and is not caused by roses. In fact, flowers of any kind very rarely cause allergy.

Goldenrod is a prime cause of hay fever.

No, it is not. This flower for generations has been falsely accused of causing hay fever. It may be that people tend to think of goldenrod and ragweed as members of the same family or even as the same plant, since in some parts of the country they tend to grow in the same place at the same time. Flowers, including goldenrod, do not cause hay fever; ragweed pollen and pollen of many other weeds *do* cause hay fever.

The most serious effect of nasal allergy is that it nearly always leads to asthma.

False. Although children with nasal allergy will occasionally develop asthma, much more often they will *not*. In fact, most cases of childhood asthma begin along with or before nasal allergy.

If a child's parents are both asthmatic, she's almost sure to have asthma too.

No. She's certainly likely to inherit an allergic tendency, but not the specific allergy. She *may* get asthma, but she may instead get nasal allergy, skin eruptions from cat dander, or any of a variety of allergic reactions—or *none*.

Asthma is not a serious disease, because no one dies from it.

Between 2,000 and 4,000 persons (mainly adults) of the 8 to 9 million afflicted die from asthma each year. Even with such a low mortality rate, asthma can cause physical suffering, emotional strain on patient and family, social problems, and economic burdens.

Asthma and the other allergies are the most widespread chronic diseases of childhood and are indeed serious.

Most asthma is the result of a poor mother-child relationship.

Pure myth. Asthma is the result of allergic tendencies and allergens. A supportive mother may help her child live with his symptoms better than an emotionally distraught mother (or father), but it's just not true that the mother can "cause" asthma, even though she's frequently found guilty in the psychological literature.

Asthma is all in the mind anyway.

No, it's not. Emotions may trigger existing asthma, but emotions do not cause asthma or other allergies. Allergens and irritants do.

Wheezing in children confirms a diagnosis of asthma.

Not always. Wheezing can be caused not only by asthma but also by choking on objects or food, by tuberculosis, by cystic fibrosis, by congenital narrowing of the air tubes, and by tumors (primarily in adults). A physician must consider wheezing along with other symptoms, the child's medical history, and other diagnostic procedures.

Asthmatic youngsters should avoid strenuous activity such as baseball or tennis but may participate in long-distance running.

No, the reverse is true. Nearly all children with asthma can and should participate in sports and games up to their capacity. Most tolerate athletics that require short bursts of activity, but *not* extended periods of strenuous exertion such as long-distance running or soccer.

Poison ivy or poison oak rash should not be washed; washing spreads the rash.

Another common misconception. Bathing may spread the fluid that oozes out of blisters, but this does not spread the rash. Skip the traditional strong soap cleansing, but bathe the exposed skin with a pure, gentle soap and wash the exposed clothes to eliminate the oleoresin that triggered the reaction.

If an allergic child gets through adolescence without having poison ivy reactions, he can be considered immune.

No, exposure to allergens can take place for months and years before producing a reaction (suddenly, it seems). Many middle-aged adults with allergic tendencies learn this the hard way by having a first case of poison ivy rash after a lifetime of being considered immune.

3. Nasal Allergy: Hay Fever and Related Miseries

Mention the word *allergy* and most people envision the stereotypical hay fever sufferer—red eyes, runny nose, explosive sneezes, exhaustion. Small wonder. Hay fever is by far the most common respiratory allergy, afflicting more than 5 million children (out of a total 6 million with nasal allergy) in the United States.

It is not the only nasal allergy affecting children, however. "Nasal allergy" is a descriptive term for several upper respiratory allergies, including hay fever.

The term *hay fever* is actually a misnomer. When the term was first used in England, it was thought that the syndrome was caused by haying, because the symptoms most often cropped up at that time of year, but in fact hay has no effect on them. *Fever* was used as a general term for illness, rather than as a specific term for an elevated temperature. More properly, the condition is called "seasonal allergic rhinitis," which simply means an allergic inflammation of the nose during certain seasons of the year. Nonetheless, the term *hay fever* has amazing staying power and is still in widespread use. You also may hear it called "rose fever," which is the same seasonal condition, first thought to be caused by exposure to flowering roses (which it is not).

Nasal allergy is so common in children that unfortunately it may be taken far too lightly. The hay fever sufferer is frequently dismissed as a comic character, an amusing sniffler overreacting to a summer cold or a mangy cat. Even concerned parents, while not amused by their child and his hay fever, too often consider the symptoms a normal part of growing up or part of a long summer cold that can be safely ignored.

Hay fever is neither normal nor a cold. (Summer colds that "last until the first freeze" are not colds.) A nasal allergy can be mild and just occasionally bothersome, but it should not be ignored. And moderate or severe nasal allergy can be an extremely stressful condition. It can leave your child physically spent and emotionally drained. It can interfere with school, work, play, sleep, eating, all the activities of daily living. It can transform your cheerful child into an irritable, manipulating terror.

Nasal allergy behaves differently in different individuals, and treatment must be varied accordingly. In general, the outlook is optimistic. Today, there are many helpful measures that can be taken if necessary—more now than there were even ten to twenty years ago. This chapter describes the important recommendations, both new and time-proven.

What Is Nasal Allergy?

Nasal allergy is a noncommunicable condition that begins when an allergic individual repeatedly inhales certain airborne substances (allergens) to which she has an allergic sensitivity. The symptoms that result are essentially an overreaction or an altered reaction of the body's immune system, the body's defense against "foreign" invaders.

The major nasal allergies in children are: both seasonal and perennial allergies, nonallergic rhinitis (included because of similar symptoms), and vasomotor rhinitis.

Seasonal nasal allergy (sometimes called "seasonal allergic rhinitis"). This is commonly known as hay fever or rose fever. The condition is marked by inflammation of the upper respiratory tract, runny nose, itching and tearing eyes, wracking sneezes, sniffling, and snorting. (See "Symptoms and Complications," later in this chapter.) The condition is the result of exposure to plant pollens or mold spores and is definitely tied to the seasons when the pollens and spores are present.

Perennial nasal allergy (sometimes called "perennial allergic rhinitis"). This condition is similar to seasonal nasal allergy, often with identical symptoms, but is strung out over months and sometimes years. It is not necessarily tied to seasonal changes and it is not caused by exposure to pollens and outdoor molds but to house dust, animal dander, and other year-round allergens. If your child has perennial nasal allergy, he may be bothered one day and not the next and his ups and downs may be harder to explain than the pollen-linked seasonal nasal allergy, or hay fever.

Nonallergic rhinitis. Technically this relatively rare condition does not belong in the nasal allergy category. It is included because the symptoms are the same as nasal allergy, although skin tests and blood tests do not demonstrate an IgE-mediated allergy. The cause of nonallergic rhinitis remains unknown, but it is treated as though it were an allergy.

Vasomotor rhinitis. Sometimes called "intrinsic rhinitis" or "stress rhinitis," vasomotor rhinitis is not a true allergy, although the symptoms can be similar to those of nasal allergy. Rhinitis simply means inflammation of the linings of the nose—swelling (congestion) and secretion of mucus. In allergic children, the rhinitis is caused by an allergic reaction; in nonallergic children it can be caused by a vasomotor reaction that is acquired, not inherited. Or the same person can suffer from both allergic and vasomotor rhinitis.

Vasomotor means motor or physical control of the blood vessels. The blood vessels in the nose of people who acquire vasomotor rhinitis will tend to react to such stimuli as a sudden change of temperature, smoke or smog, strong odors, or a change in humidity by expanding or contracting, resulting in the symptoms of rhinitis. While everyone is somewhat sensitive to irritants like smog or fumes, those with vasomotor rhinitis are overly sensitive.

Vasomotor rhinitis and allergies are apt to occur in the same person, so any persistent symptoms should be brought to your doctor's attention.

Although nasal allergy most frequently begins after

a child is at least two years old, it does occur in infants.
In younger children, the reaction more often results
from food allergies than from inhaled allergens, although the symptoms are the same. More on that when
we discuss food allergies in chapter 5.

Why the Allergic Reaction Varies

What really goes on during the allergic reaction—why
your child flares up over a substance that another child
doesn't even notice—is still not fully understood. But
medical researchers have a far better idea now than
they used to.

As explained in chapter 1, the allergic reaction is
an antigen-antibody reaction. An antigen is a foreign
substance that sets off the body's immune system,
causing the often violent symptoms that accompany
the body's defense against invasion. When an antigen
causes an allergic reaction, it's called an allergen. If
your child has hay fever, she was first exposed several
times to an allergen, say ragweed pollen, without experiencing the symptoms of hay fever. After repeated
exposures, her immune system (her body's defense
system) starts to produce specific antibodies to counteract specific allergens—special antibodies that react
only to ragweed pollen, in this case, but not to grass
pollen or any other potential allergen. When the antibody reacts with the allergen, it produces the allergic
reaction. (See Appendix A, "The Allergic Reaction,"
for more details.)

Of course, this explanation is greatly simplified.
The complex, only partially understood allergic reaction involves a lot of variables. The severity of your

child's allergies can vary greatly, even from day to day.

The *concentration* of the allergen in the air is often a factor. Hay fever sufferers nearly always can tell you when the pollen count is high, if you can't already tell by observing their heightened symptoms. By the same token, a child who is allergic to house dust will fare much better in a relatively clean home than he will in a musty, dusty one—and so on.

The *duration* of exposure is important too. Some hay fever sufferers have a fairly low reaction to the first few days of a pollen season, even if the pollen count is high. But after weeks or just several days of exposure, the nose can become more sensitive and may react markedly to a day when the pollen count is low. Similarly, a child who is allergic to cats may be able to spend the afternoon at a cat-owning friend's house, but after a week there she'd be in trouble.

Nasal allergy reactions can start suddenly, even though your child may have been exposed to an allergen many times without previous reactions. Symptoms may seem to appear abruptly, right out of the blue, but chances are that your child's system had been building up to such a reaction for some time. Still, if your child has lived at peace with his pet dog for years, for example, and suddenly develops perennial nasal allergy from inhaling dog dander, it's an upsetting experience.

"Will My Child Outgrow It?"

Maybe. Allergists feel that, in general, the prognosis for children with nasal allergy is good and improving slightly each year. However, it's virtually impossible to predict the outcome of an individual case, even though a certain percentage of children do outgrow nasal allergy. What percentage? Estimates range from a low of 5 to 10 percent to almost 50 percent by late adolescence.

Some children will retain nasal allergy into adulthood. Some will outgrow it. Others will outgrow it only to acquire another allergy—a more common outcome than for the child to remain allergy-free. Certainly the chances of your child outgrowing his nasal allergy or at least getting the symptoms under control for near-normal living are improved if the condition is recognized and treated. Nearly all young patients are helped dramatically if the involved allergen is identified and their exposure to it cut back. Other youngsters benefit greatly from medications or immunotherapy (allergy shots). The arsenal of treatment weapons grows every year, in both quantity and quality.

One widespread worry of parents whose child has nasal allergy is that he'll inevitably acquire asthma as he grows older. Not so. Most allergists now feel that the traditional fear of nasal allergy (hay fever especially) leading to asthma is overplayed. It is far from inevitable, because in most children who have both nasal allergy and asthma, the asthma developed first or the conditions developed together. And, while it's true that some children with nasal allergy may develop very mild symptoms of asthma, this does not mean they will get full asthma attacks later. (See chapter 4, "Bronchial Asthma.")

Symptoms and Complications

If your child has had nasal allergy for some time, the symptoms may be all too familiar. But in the beginning, the disease is not that obvious, even if you have reason to suspect it.

When your child is still an infant, before she's developed nasal allergy, you may encounter feeding difficulties like her sniffling and snorting at the bottle or breast from breathing problems, and breaking out with eczema or hives on introduction of new foods. These are strong indicators that your baby will develop some kind of allergy later in life—not necessarily nasal allergy.

In such infants, perennial nasal allergy may begin in two-year-olds and seasonal allergy (hay fever) usually not before age three. In either case, the first symptoms probably will be similar to those of a common cold—without the fever. Nasal allergies can sneak up on you. If your child has two or three extended bouts of "colds" or several weeks of the same "cold," take her to your doctor. It's normal for her to have six to eight colds a year but not normal to have a "cold" that lasts longer than a week or ten days at the most without complications.

Early symptoms. A child with nasal allergy usually has a runny, congested nose that makes him sniffle, snort, and sneeze, and an intense itch in his nose and on the roof of his mouth. He may also have teary, reddened eyes and a mucous cough that brings nothing up.

The mucous membrane lining of the throat, mouth,

and particularly the nose becomes drenched with clear mucous discharge, resulting in the runny nose. The cough is from a "tickle" in the nose-throat passage. Dry, hacking coughs are more usually associated with asthma.

With the appearance of early symptoms, you can do some very important detective work on your own to help your physician make a diagnosis. After all, who sees your child more than you? Nasal allergy can mimic other conditions, such as a cold, flu, or chronic sinus infection. It may take close observation of the symptoms to figure out what is actually causing them. Here are some things to watch for:

If his symptoms are intense in the morning and evening but not during the afternoon, suspect nasal allergy. If his symptoms occur during a heavy pollen season in your area and not during the off seasons, suspect hay fever (seasonal rhinitis). The sneeze pattern is often hay fever's calling card, although it's not quite as common in children as in adults. If your child sneezes in the morning when he's getting up, and especially if he has a string of ten to twenty sneezes that leave him exhausted, suspect hay fever. If his sneezes are sporadic, with no pattern and no seasonal variation, suspect *perennial* rhinitis, which is much less common.

These are common early symptoms, but in life nothing is quite that simple; certainly allergies are not. Your child may well have nasal allergy *and* a common cold. He may have some symptoms but not all. He may react very mildly to the suspected allergens or much more violently than expected, and so on. The following comparisons may be helpful:

How to Tell Nasal Allergy
from the Common Cold

Nasal allergy (allergic reaction)	*Common cold* (viral or secondary bacterial infection)
Symptoms persist	Symptoms usually are gone within seven days
Rarely with fever over 100° F	More frequently with fever over 100° F
Sneezing frequent in early morning, in series, persistent	Sneezing usually just early in the seven-day course
Usually intense itching of nose, mouth, eyes	Seldom intense itching
Lining of nose and mouth usually glistening, pale, swollen ("boggy") on doctor's exam	Lining of nose and mouth red from inflammation on doctor's exam

These comparisons do not constitute a diagnosis, which must be made by your doctor, but they may help you sort out symptoms.

By the way, with either nasal allergy or the common cold, most allergists and many pediatricians recommend sending the child to school unless he's really feeling sick. A leading medical school allergist says, "I feel strongly that children should not be kept home if they have allergy symptoms that mimic cold symptoms, or even if they have a cold. Allergies are not contagious, and as for the common cold, by the time a child has the symptoms, he already has contaminated every one he's going to contaminate. Besides, he'll

probably be less rambunctious in school than he would
be at home. If a child with allergy or cold symptoms
has a fever—anything over 100° F—or earache and
really feels sick, keep him home."

Later symptoms. Nosebleeds are fairly common in
children who have nasal allergy. Usually this does not
indicate anything serious. Your child probably rubs
her nose frequently to relieve the itch. Since the blood
vessels in the nose are swollen, they are prone to bleed
when rubbed. When this happens, have your child lie
down for a few minutes and pinch the tip of her nose
between thumb and index finger until the bleeding
stops, or you can do it for her. This nearly always
works with very little discomfort; she's probably
breathing through her mouth anyway. If nosebleeds
recur frequently, see your doctor.

Headache sometimes accompanies nasal allergy. It
usually involves the sinuses and causes a dull pain
across the forehead. Younger children have fewer sinus
headaches because some of their sinuses are still im-
mature and don't contribute to headache. Your allergic
child may seem to have symptoms of sinusitis (inflammation of the sinus cavities), but the sinus headaches can also be caused by nasal allergy alone without
actual inflammation, because the congestion of allergy
blocks sinus drainage, building up pressure in the sinuses. If your child can't shake the headache, see your
doctor. And check with your doctor *before* you give
your child any medicine for the headache; he may not
recommend aspirin. (See chapter 4, under "Nonallergens and Asthma.")

Have you heard of the "allergic salute"? If not, you
probably will. It describes the child's use of the palm
of her hand to rub the tip of her nose upward. It's a

habitual attempt to relieve the itch and get rid of congestion. The allergic crease is one result—a horizontal crease across the bridge of the nose that appears if rubbing continues for a long period of time.

"Rabbit nose" is a descriptive phrase for another habitual movement. Some nasal allergy sufferers twitch their nose continually, much as a rabbit does, in an effort to clear the congestion.

Breathing through the mouth is another way children compensate for clogged noses. Children seldom resort to mouth breathing early in their nasal allergy, but eventually do it unconsciously whenever the nose becomes too congested. Nothing is dangerously wrong with this, although the mouth and gums quickly become dry. In the long run, chronic mouth breathing can somewhat alter the facial features and create dental problems such as maxillary overbite, but this takes several years.

It also takes a year or two of the disease to produce "allergic shiners," (dark puffy crescents under the eyes caused by chronic fluid "pooling") often seen when a child gets up in the morning. She may also look pale, although she is not anemic. These are classic nasal allergy signs. Irritability from loss of sleep and frustration often accompany the allergic shiners. (See the discussion of "Tension-fatigue syndrome" in chapter 8.)

Some loss of taste and smell is common with nasal allergy. This is more of a problem—at least recognized more often—in older children. The swollen mucosal lining and resulting congestion interfere with normal smell and taste. When the congestion clears up, these senses return to normal.

Serious complications. Some temporary hearing loss

is not uncommon with nasal allergy in children. Permanent hearing impairment, although rare, is the most serious complication, so your doctor will routinely check your child's hearing.

But if you notice hearing problems, call them to your doctor's attention. Your child may have temporary hearing difficulties without being aware of them. Does he turn the television set up way too loud, or miss conversations? These may be your only clues.

Most hearing problems associated with nasal allergy are caused by serous otitis media—the accumulation of fluid in the middle ear behind the ear drum. The condition seldom occurs in children older than age ten. Fluid builds up in the ear because the mucosal linings, swollen by the allergy, block the auditory tube (eustachion tube). The auditory tube connects the ear and back of the throat for drainage and pressure regulation.

Serous otitis media sometimes causes a feeling of pressure or fullness in the middle ear, but in other cases the child feels little if any discomfort. The fluid behind the eardrum often is clear and nonirritating, so a great deal can accumulate without causing any pain. Allergists warn, however, that the accumulated fluid may become infected, which in turn may lead to a serious ear infection. So if you *suspect* hearing problems in your allergic child, see your doctor promptly.

The symptoms described above are good indications of nasal allergy in the majority of children. But your child is unique. How nasal allergy affects her, if at all, depends on her special qualities. Work with your doctor to arrive at a firm diagnosis.

Common Hay Fever Allergens

Children (and adults) can be allergic to almost anything, but certain substances are much more likely than others to provoke allergic reactions. Hay fever (seasonal nasal allergy) proves the point.

Airborne pollens and mold spores are far and away the most common causes of hay fever. The pollens are microscopic bits, smaller than the width of a human hair. As certain trees, weeds, and grasses enter the season to fertilize their seeds, they give off millions of pollen bits to be carried by the wind and deposited on female plants of the same species. Only one in millions is carried to its proper destination, so nature sees to it that plenty are launched.

Daily pollen counts are reported in some areas of the country during peak seasons. The higher the count, the greater the concentration of pollen in the air, and the more intense the allergic person's reaction is likely to be. But if the person is highly allergic to a certain pollen, it doesn't take a high count to bring on the symptoms. It's possible for a count as low as twenty (twenty grains per cubic meter, or slightly over a cubic yard of air) to cause symptoms in some highly sensitive patients.

Mold spores too can cause hay fever. Outdoors, molds grow widely, often on grains and grasses, on the leaves of trees and bushes, and in the soil around the roots of many plants. The spores — mold "seeds" — are smaller than pollen and easily carried by the wind. Seasons of mold spore reaction generally are longer than pollen seasons.

Molds are not nearly as common a cause of hay fever as are pollens, but they can cause just as severe a reaction. Often they combine with a pollen allergy. Your child may get through a pollen season with just mild symptoms, only to have some symptoms persist for weeks longer because they're caused by mold spores. The first frost stops most pollen from forming, but it takes longer to stop molds.

Your doctor will tell you what trees, weeds, grasses, and molds are common in your area—at least those that affect your child. Generally, they follow this pattern:

East of the Rockies. East of the Rockies the most common allergen causing hay fever is Eastern ragweed pollen (not to be confused with the much-maligned goldenrod, which is innocent). Eastern ragweed grows nearly everywhere east of the Rockies and pollinates between mid-August and mid- or late September. This is the big one. It accounts for up to 75 percent of cases of hay fever in this area. Other weeds that can cause hay fever include sheep sorrel and English plantain.

Various grasses can cause it, including sweet vernal, Bermuda, timothy, orchard, Johnson, Kentucky blue, and redtop, which pollinate generally in late spring in the Midwest and East.

So can trees, including maple, elm, poplar, alder, cottonwood, ash, walnut, hickory, sycamore, and mulberry. They pollinate generally in early spring in the Midwest and East.

West of the Rockies and the Southwest. The pattern here is markedly different from the East. In Texas, for example, mountain cedar can cause hay fever in midwinter.

Throughout the Southwest and West, even where Eastern ragweed is sparse or absent, Western ragweed, Russian thistle (tumbleweed), sage, and amaranth are widespread. Salt bush, dock-plantain, chenopod, kochia, and certain other plants are allergy-causing in their pollen season, but are less widespread; they tend to be heavily concentrated in distinct parts of Western states, even in certain counties. Other weeds that can cause hay fever include careless weed, pigweed, burning bush, lamb's quarter, cockleweed, and marsh elder.

The list of weeds, grasses, and trees at fault can go on and on by geographical location, but the important question—What is producing hay fever here?—can best be answered by your doctor.

The pollen calendar on pages 34 to 37 gives a national picture of the most common pollens. As you will see, no area in the continental United States is free of pollen allergens at all times. Some states, on paper, look better than others, but if you're thinking of moving to help your child and her hay fever, think again. And talk it over with your doctor. Most allergists never recommend a move to cure or improve an allergy. Any possible short-term advantages probably would be offset by long-term disadvantages. Your child probably would trade one allergy for another.

If you moved from the East to California, your allergic child might find relief from Eastern ragweed allergy only to pick up Bermuda grass allergy. Moving from the West Coast to the Midwest or East involves the same sort of tradeoff. An allergic child may (or may *not*) experience a few months of relatively symptom-free living before developing a sensitivity to the predominant local allergen. And the trauma of a move

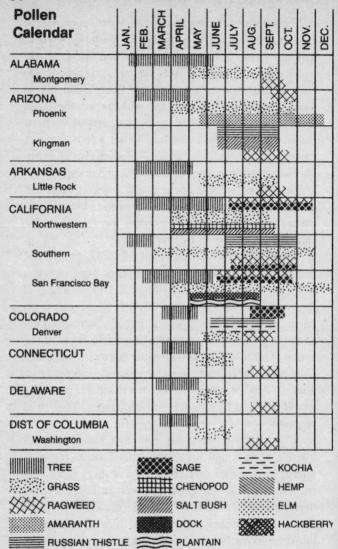

34

Pollen Calendar

	JAN.	FEB.	MARCH	APRIL	MAY	JUNE	JULY	AUG.	SEPT.	OCT.	NOV.	DEC.

ALABAMA
Montgomery

ARIZONA
Phoenix

Kingman

ARKANSAS
Little Rock

CALIFORNIA
Northwestern

Southern

San Francisco Bay

COLORADO
Denver

CONNECTICUT

DELAWARE

DIST. OF COLUMBIA
Washington

‖‖‖‖ TREE	✕✕✕ SAGE	- - - KOCHIA
⠐⠄ GRASS	⊞⊞ CHENOPOD	⟋⟋ HEMP
✕✕ RAGWEED	⟋⟋ SALT BUSH	⠐⠄ ELM
▓▓ AMARANTH	● DOCK	✕✕✕ HACKBERRY
≡≡ RUSSIAN THISTLE	≈≈ PLANTAIN	

Pollen calendar. From J. M. Sheldon, R. G. Lovell, K. P. Matthews, *A Manual of Clinical Allergy*, 2d ed. (W. B. Saunders, 1967), pp. 342–343. Used by permission.

	JAN.	FEB.	MARCH	APRIL	MAY	JUNE	JULY	AUG.	SEPT.	OCT.	NOV.	DEC.

FLORIDA
Miami

Tampa

GEORGIA
Atlanta

IDAHO
Southern

ILLINOIS
Chicago

INDIANA
Indianapolis

IOWA
Ames

KANSAS
Wichita

KENTUCKY
Louisville

LOUISIANA
New Orleans

MAINE

MARYLAND
Baltimore

MASSACHUSETTS
Boston

MICHIGAN
Detroit

MINNESOTA
Minneapolis

	JAN.	FEB.	MARCH	APRIL	MAY	JUNE	JULY	AUG.	SEPT.	OCT.	NOV.	DEC.
MISSISSIPPI Vicksburg												
MISSOURI St. Louis Kansas City												
MONTANA Miles City												
NEBRASKA Omaha												
NEVADA Reno												
NEW HAMPSHIRE												
NEW JERSEY												
NEW MEXICO Roswell												
NEW YORK New York City												
NORTH CAROLINA Raleigh												
NORTH DAKOTA Fargo												
OHIO Cleveland												
OKLAHOMA Oklahoma City												
OREGON Portland												
East of Cascade Mountains												

	JAN.	FEB.	MARCH	APRIL	MAY	JUNE	JULY	AUG.	SEPT.	OCT.	NOV.	DEC.
PENNSYLVANIA												
RHODE ISLAND												
SOUTH CAROLINA Charleston												
SOUTH DAKOTA												
TENNESSEE Nashville												
TEXAS Dallas												
Brownsville												
UTAH Salt Lake City												
VERMONT												
VIRGINIA Richmond												
WASHINGTON Seattle												
Eastern												
WEST VIRGINIA												
WISCONSIN Madison												
WYOMING												

certainly does not help a child with hay fever—or his
family.

A *temporary* change—a holiday or vacation in another part of the country—is another matter. It can
be a wonderfully revitalizing experience for the whole
family. Don't remain housebound. Check with your
doctor for tips and ideas and enjoy the change.

The Perennial Nasal Allergy Allergens

If your child has perennial nasal allergy, the culprit
allergen is probably lurking in your house. The major
causes are house dust, animal dander, and indoor mold
and mildew. House dust is such a common allergen
that some allergists consider this the most important
single question to ask a patient who may have nasal
allergy: "Do you have trouble with dust?"

The house dust in question is not the fine-dirt variety tracked in from the lawn or street, but the tiny
specks you see in shafts of sunlight. It's a combination
of many indoor substances that can cause allergy. The
mixture varies, but may contain bits of fabric fibers;
feathers; mold and fungus in humid months; animal
dander; disintegrated stuffing from overstuffed furniture, stuffed toys, pillows, and mattresses; bits of drapery and carpet material; and especially kapok and cotton
lint. The stereotypical Victorian drawing room is the
epitome of an allergenic room, with its old drapery
hangings, dark rugs, dust-catching bric-a-brac, dusty
(and often musty) old books, the family parrot in a
dusty cage by the dusty hearth, and so on.

If it's not all that pleasant to realize that these materials are probably floating around your house, wait:

There's more. One ingredient is common to nearly all house dust—the dust mite, a very small spiderlike creature that feeds on tiny bits of human and animal dander and transforms house dust into a primary allergen. *Dermatophagoides pteronyssinus*, the long name for the small insect, means "skin eater."

If you have a pet—nearly any kind that does not crawl or swim—the pet becomes a prime suspect. Most allergists consider a pet guilty until proven innocent. Long-hair or short-hair makes no difference; it's the dander, the tiny bits of dead skin shed constantly by the animal, that causes the allergies. Birds can be as bad as furry animals for some children.

Other substances—irritants—that can worsen your child's perennial nasal allergy include strong fumes such as paint smells; perfumes and other cosmetics; cigarette smoke; wood dust from a basement workbench; mothballs; and many household cleaners.

Diagnosis of Nasal Allergy

If you suspect nasal allergy in your child, take her to see your doctor. And be prepared for questions and more questions. Doctors rely primarily on the history of your child's illness and on the family history for a diagnosis, plus a physical examination, laboratory tests of blood and mucus, X-rays, and skin tests when indicated.

Most doctors will begin by asking for the following information, generally in this order:

1. Severity. How bad is it? Is your child just sniffling a bit or is she really sick and worn out from the condition?

2. Frequency. How often does your child have the symptoms? Every day? Twice a week? Once a month?
3. Seasons. Are the symptoms present during a certain season of the year but not year-round?
4. Probable allergens or irritants. How does your child react to house dust? Colds? Animals? Foods? Exposure to grasses, weeds, trees?

That, of course, is just the outline. The questions are likely to be numerous and quite detailed. Some doctors may ask you to fill out an allergy questionnaire, usually before the visit.

In addition to the history, your doctor probably will examine your child to assess his general physical condition. She may concentrate on the nose, mouth, throat, eyes, and ears for telltale signs, and nearly always will check tonsils and adenoids. (Enlarged adenoids can cause mouth breathing and the condition may be confused with allergy at first. If the condition is indeed an allergy, the doctor is not likely to recommend removal of tonsils and adenoids, which will not relieve nasal allergy and should not be done for that purpose.)

Also, your doctor probably will listen carefully to your child's chest. Breathing sounds can point to many conditions, including bronchitis, pneumonia, and early signs of bronchial asthma.

And more questions. Is your child unusually irritable? Are his symptoms worse when the furnace is on? Does he have a bedroom of his own? What kind of furniture? A good diagnostician will at some point get very personal, even asking you how clean your house is, or at least your child's bedroom. Sometimes it's hard not to feel a little defensive about these issues. Keep in mind that the doctor doesn't want to criticize you; she just wants to discover the source of your child's distress.

Laboratory tests. Most physicians will not use laboratory tests to diagnose nasal allergy in children if the condition is strongly suggested by the symptoms and the child is otherwise healthy. If there is a question about your child's suspected allergy, lab tests can help. Commonly, blood and mucus are checked for eosinophils, special white blood cells that increase in number during an allergic reaction. They are often called "allergy cells." Different white blood cells, neutrophils, increase if there is an *infectious* disease rather than an *allergic* condition present.

Your doctor may order a urinalysis to help rule out other illnesses. And he may do X-ray studies of your child's sinuses to be certain there is no infection (sinusitis) or obstruction from enlarged adenoids. Special X-rays may help your physician check for polyps in your child's nose, although these are rare in children and only result from a lingering allergy. Polyps are small, noncancerous swellings in the nose that look like a small grape with the skin off.

Do not be concerned if your doctor skips X-rays at first and later wants some done. This doesn't automatically mean that your child's condition is worse than he thought. Some physicians wait until after a few weeks of antihistamine and decongestant treatment in the hope that some shrinkage and drainage will result in sharper, more useful X-ray films.

It's fairly common for a physician to order further testing of your child's hearing also. On the first visit, your physician may check hearing by audiometry but he may want you to see a specialist for more complete evaluation. It's time well spent. Temporary hearing loss can undermine your child's self-confidence in school, in the family, and among her peers.

Skin tests. Skin tests usually are performed by allergists rather than pediatricians or family doctors, because interpretation of the results is sometimes complicated. The allergist will choose the likely allergens to test in your child. There's no point in skin testing for just anything. Since the procedure is time-consuming and fairly expensive, it is not done routinely, nor is it often done in very young children. Most allergists say the child should be age three or older.

Skin testing is not a painful procedure. Reassure your child, if he's to be tested. Very diluted samples of suspected allergens are injected into the skin or touched onto the skin and scratched. If the child is allergic to one or more of the tested allergens, he will have a reaction within about fifteen minutes. The reaction, called "wheal and flare," looks somewhat like a mosquito bite. If there's no reaction, the skin looks normal.

What determines whether or not your child should be skin tested? Age, extent of disability, and difficulty of diagnosis. If your child is younger than age three or responding well to treatment, skin tests are seldom even considered. If he's having persistent problems that interfere with sleep, school, and other daily activities, skin tests may be in order to help your doctor plan further treatment.

In some cases, allergists may use new blood tests to test for allergens rather than doing skin tests, especially when looking for food allergens. The most commonly used new blood test is the radioallergosorbent test (RAST), described in Appendix B.

Treatment of Nasal Allergy

There is no "best" way of treating nasal allergy. All of the options have their uses, but not all will be right for your child. The best one for your child is not necessarily the one that controls the most symptoms, but the one that allows her to live the most normal life—without severe symptoms *or* side effects. A treatment that causes more problems than it cures is no help at all.

Basically, there are three approaches to treatment of nasal allergy: remove the offending allergen, control the symptoms with medications, use immunotherapy (allergy shots). If you can eliminate the allergen, your child won't need the other two. In other cases, controlling the symptoms with medications may be all that is needed. In persistent cases, immunotherapy can sometimes produce dramatic improvement.

There *is* one other treatment option: no treatment at all. If the condition is very mild, your doctor may recommend against *any* treatment or further testing, and just see the child on regular checkups. It's possible to complicate a very mild allergic condition by treating when no treatment is necessary.

Eliminating the allergens. Removing the allergens that cause the disease is without question the most effective treatment. This fact seems obvious, but you might be surprised at how often it is bypassed in the futile rush for a quick cure or a magic pill. Also, some parents balk at what they anticipate will be a major upheaval in their style of living—tossing out a houseful of furniture and buying chrome and plastic, moving to a mountain top, sterilizing all objects the child may touch, and taking on the role of a ministering angel.

Most physicians, including nearly all allergists, today agree that the object of treatment is to improve the quality of your child's life, not to control every single symptom. So an intense, twenty-four-hour surveillance with you and your spouse performing heroic feats of care is not the right approach. This overresponse can leave you and your child hanging on the ropes, and such emotional exhaustion is *not* in anyone's best interests.

Few parents can or do totally overhaul the home environment when nasal allergy is diagnosed in their child, but nearly all find they can do a great deal of good with a few simple changes. Remember, the type of change and care you and your doctor agree on is not just for a day or two, but for longer, sometimes far longer periods of time. The plan has to be something your doctor can approve and, just as important, something that will work for your family.

An allergist reports, "Too often the mother of a child with perennial nasal allergy will come in feeling guilty because she missed one morning of damp-mopping the whole downstairs. That kind of tension is destructive. Maybe she thought I expect that of her, but I certainly don't. A detailed regimen of house cleaning that leaves a parent exhausted and guilty is counterproductive."

If your child has hay fever (seasonal nasal allergy),

there is, of course, only so much you can do to change his hostile environment. You can't totally eliminate pollens and molds, but when you know what your child is allergic to, common sense will help you cut down his exposure. As he grows, he too can figure out ways to avoid the offending allergens.

Certainly during high pollen seasons, he can avoid walking through fields of grasses and weeds if he's allergic to them. And he can stay away from gardening and lawn-mowing, which is one preventive measure most youngsters have no trouble complying with. Other than avoiding camping trips and picnics at the height of the pollen season when he's apt to be the most uncomfortable, plan your activities to include him as you would any other child.

If your child is really uncomfortable it's prudent to keep him inside as much as possible during high pollen days—usually the sunny, breezy, hot ones when the outdoors beckons. It's almost a necessity to have at least your child's bedroom air-conditioned so you can close the outside doors and windows when necessary *and* the outside air vent on the air conditioner.

If your child is extremely allergic to outdoor mold, she probably should not be around orchards, vegetable gardens, or newly plowed fields any more than necessary, and mowing the lawn may not be a good idea either. However, if she is mildly or moderately allergic to molds and has a chance for a trip to the country, the trip is probably worth the chance of some aggravation. Most allergists feel that letting the child enjoy a country outing, with the help of prescribed medications, is far better than overprotecting by keeping her home.

If your child has *perennial* nasal allergy with its

unpredictable ups and downs, there are many things you can do that will help. There's a good chance she will be allergic to more than one allergen, and a very good chance that one of them will be house dust. That situation you can make much more tolerable. The section on "Your Child's Environment" in chapter 8 describes how to cut down on house dust and mold without turning your house into a hospital. Your doctor may have additional suggestions.

If your doctor gives you a battle plan that would mean converting your house from top to bottom, talk it over with him. Ask him what the most important steps are. It's vital, after all, that you can make the plan work. A total-house program that's not adhered to is worse than no plan at all. And in the planning, be sure you allow some time for the new routine to work. You won't notice spectacular changes in your child overnight; rather, you'll probably notice some gradual improvement after a month or so.

If a family pet is identified as a source of your child's perennial nasal allergy, obviously you've got a problem. This can happen after your child has spent several trouble-free, affectionate years with the pet too. The blanket rule is simply stated: No pets should be in a home where there are people allergic to them. One implication is easily followed: Do not go out and buy a new pet. The other implication—getting rid of the present pet—has to be up for discussion.

The discussion, by the way, should always include your child, who's at the center of the dilemma. If there are siblings who are also attached to the pet, they should take part in the decision making too. This has to be a judgment call. Weigh the probable benefits of giving away the pet against the emotional trauma such a move will bring. Point out the consequences, but discuss alternatives to total separation. Often a compromise is in the best interests of the child and the pet. She may not mind a few more sniffles if she can keep her dog.

One possibility is to allow the dog or cat to stay in the garage or in a dog house, but not in the house and especially not in your child's room. This adjustment can be difficult for a housepet; if the animal is not used to staying outside, ask your veterinarian how to make the transition easier. Other possibilities are varied (your veterinarian may have some suggestions), but the point is, try not to leave your child emotionally scarred by total and immediate removal of a beloved pet, especially if he is an only child. Even if it's doubtful that a compromise will work (if you live in a small city apartment, for example) *always* discuss the situation with the child before getting rid of the animal. Sudden disposal of a family pet can make a small child fearful that he too is easily dispensable.

If your child's condition is persistent, your doctor may suggest other measures, such as installing a dehumidifier in the basement or a central air-conditioning and cleaning system with central humidification and electrostatic precipitation. But move slowly. Many of the mechanical aids, such as electrostatic precipitation and filtration units, are of undetermined worth. Most allergists feel that they may help, but there is very little solid information to back this up. Check with your doctor before you consider any such major changes. And don't worry if you can't afford them. Concentrate on the things you *can* do, which are probably much more useful.

Here again, remember that it's important to treat

the whole child, not just the allergy. It sometimes is tempting, if you can afford it, to put a great deal of time and effort into questionable electronic aids, when the time and effort could be spent in much more productive ways with your child—a short holiday trip if she's losing her pep during a pollen season, for example.

Nasal Allergy Medications

Any medications your child takes, including those you buy without a prescription and not necessarily for allergy, should be checked with your doctor the first time around. It's the best way to avoid serious side effects and problems with drug interactions (certain medicines should not be taken together), and to assure your child the most benefit.

Be sure your child understands that his allergy medicine is not going to "cure" hay fever in the same way that an antibiotic can be said to cure a bacterial pneumonia by eliminating the infection. But he can hope for some welcome relief from the symptoms, even if they are severe.

There are several categories of nasal medications: antihistamines, decongestants, and steroids.

Antihistamines. Six types of antihistamines can be used for nasal allergy: alkylamines, ethylene, diamines, ethanolamines, phenothiazines, and a miscellaneous group. So, if your child does not respond to one type, your doctor can switch to another from among the remaining five. That wide choice didn't exist a decade ago.

Antihistamines can be very effective in patients with hay fever. Perhaps three-fourths of hay fever patients who take antihistamines improve and find relief from sneezing, itching, and runny nose, but probably *not* from nasal congestion.

Your doctor probably will start the antihistamines just before a hay fever season and continue them throughout the season. That's more effective than starting them after hay fever symptoms have appeared. Also, most specialists recommend a continuing daily dosage during the pollen season, not just when a child feels the need. If the medication causes undesirable side effects, ask the doctor if the daily dosage can be adjusted so that the child can take the antihistamines without undue discomfort.

Antihistamines block the action of the chemical histamine, which in turn dries up the nose tissue. They can be increased in dosage only so far without producing adverse side effects.

Most have a common side effect, even when taken in moderate quantities: They tend to make children drowsy, although some children may instead become irritable or jumpy. Drowsiness is rare in the very young child. In the older child, it can lead to problems, particularly in school, where it can be misinterpreted as lack of interest or laziness. If your child is drowsy from antihistamines, your doctor may choose to prescribe it to be taken only at bedtime.

If your child is beginning a course of antihistamines, try to start it on a weekend so you can observe the effect while she's at home. At least start it in the evening rather than on a school day morning.

Decongestants. Nasal decongestants, alone or with

antihistamines, can help many children with nasal allergy. They shrink the swollen mucous membranes, which reduces congestion, and they help counteract some of the drowsiness often produced by anthistamines.

Decongestants can be taken orally or topically (the latter as nose drops or sprays). The most commonly prescribed decongestants are Sudafed®—also available in combination with an antihistamine in such preparations as Actifed® or Deconamine®—Fedahist® and several others. Decongestants can cause drowsiness, but are more likely to cause irritability.

If your child is to use a decongestant nasal spray or drops such as Afrin® or Neo-Synephrine®, be sure you carefully monitor the dosage. He should *not* take them more often or in greater doses than prescribed. It's a real temptation for a youngster to overdo anything that seems to work well in relieving his symptoms. Unfortunately, a child can easily become "hooked" on nasal decongestant sprays and drops. In addition, overuse can cause a severe rebound effect when the medication is stopped, often making the condition worse than it was before medication. Nasal sprays and drops are for brief use only. If they seem to be needed for longer than several days, check with your doctor.

Steroids. Recently, new topical steroid medications have become available for treatment of nasal allergy— Beconase®, Vancenase®, and Nasalide®. These medications have been shown to be very effective. They are cortisonelike and apparently without serious side effects if prescribed with caution and discretion. Steroids do have a place in the treatment of nasal allergy, principally to cut down the inflammation, but are used sparingly in children and almost never for long periods, due to the adverse side effects associated with long usage. Oral and especially injected steroids are more likely to produce adverse side effects than are the newer topical steroids.

Immunotherapy (Allergy Shots)

Immunotherapy is sometimes called hyposensitization, sometimes desensitization, and usually allergy shots by those people receiving them.

Allergy shots are administered more often to adults than to children, but if cutting down exposure and giving medications have not helped your child enough, your doctor may prescribe immunotherapy. (Some doctors prescribe immunotherapy *before* medications and turn to antihistamines and decongestants if the patient's symptoms continue to be severe, but most allergists try the medications first with children.) Most physicians don't recommend allergy shots for children younger than five years, but practice varies on this point; some will consider shots for a child as young as two or three. The children who benefit most from allergy shots are those with seasonal nasal allergy (hay fever).

Allergy shots involve the injection of the allergen your child is allergic to. Your doctor will start with a very small amount of the allergen extract and gradually, over weeks and months, increase the dose. The goal is to produce a blocking action by administering these small, tolerated amounts of the substance your child is allergic to. This blocks the allergic reaction from taking place, or at least diminishes the reaction during the next exposure. As with any other form of treatment, it does not "cure" the allergy and doesn't always work, but results are most often quite good. However, allergy shots help very little in cases of food allergy.

If your child enters a program of immunotherapy, the prime requirement is patience. The procedure involves many visits to the doctor, perhaps weekly at first until the optimal dose is reached, then once or twice a month. It's safe to say that most children don't look forward to the shots, but you have to see that they get them on schedule. After a while, the visits will get tedious, and you may feel capable of giving the shot to your child yourself to save time and money, but *don't do it*. As with any shot, there is always the rare chance of a flareup reaction—anaphylaxis—that can be serious, even life-threatening. (See chapter 7, "Allergic Emergencies.") If this rare event should occur, let it happen in the doctor's office where trained people can handle it.

Don't expect dramatic change for the first few weeks. Allergists recommend a year's program for a worthwhile immunotherapy, and some recommend two years. If you see that your child stays with the prescribed program, results often are very good and some patients obtain relief of symptoms to the point that medications are no longer needed.

4. Bronchial Asthma

Among chronic diseases of childhood, asthma is the major cause of absences from school, and severe asthma is an extremely distressing condition. The severity and frequency of asthma attacks vary from child to child, however. Some children will have just an attack or two a year and be symptom-free between episodes. Others may have an attack that lasts a week or more. The majority of children with asthma have mild to moderate cases, as is true with most chronic conditions.

If your child has asthma or you think she does, she should be under a doctor's care. But there's no need for undue anxiety. Bronchial asthma is treatable and in virtually no cases does it leave any lung damage. Medications and other forms of treatment are very effective, both in preventing and in subduing attacks.

Some parents confuse asthma with emphysema.

Fortunately, they are not the same disease. With asthma there is usually no permanent damage to the lungs, while with emphysema there is progressive, irreversible damage to portions of the lung.

This comparison in no way justifies being lax about asthma. If left untreated it can seriously affect a child's growth and development, schooling, and overall well-being. Much of the damage can be averted if you get proper care for your child as soon as she has symptoms of asthma.

The severity of an asthma attack varies from a mild cough to extreme respiratory distress. Obstruction of the airways causes shortness of breath, and when this is severe it may produce a terrifying sense of suffocation. That terror can feed the attack and worsen it.

An asthma attack in your child also can leave *you* shaken the first time. Once you learn how to help your child through the gasping for breath and the wheezing of an acute attack, you'll be less harried and more helpful. Remember that in most children the asthma is *controlled* if properly diagnosed and treated.

Have you heard that asthma can be outgrown? Some self-styled experts preach that you can ignore asthma because your child will outgrow it. Don't believe them. Some children do outgrow asthma, but many do not, and a great many of those who do need help in the meantime. About half of all adults with asthma first became asthmatic when they were children, so obviously not all children outgrow the condition.

It's practically impossible to predict the course of your child's asthma, but generally prospects are much brighter now than a generation ago, thanks to new medications and treatment methods. In general, the milder the asthma, the more likely it will improve when the child reaches puberty. Unfortunately, it may recur in some children who show good improvement for a while.

All childhood asthma should be diagnosed and treated if necessary. It shouldn't be necessary to emphasize this, but a few parents are swayed by the "she'll outgrow it" advice. Whether or not she later grows out of it, every asthmatic child deserves good treatment during childhood.

What Is Bronchial Asthma?

Bronchial asthma affects the bronchial tubes in the lungs. Like other allergies, it is caused by an abnormal reaction of the immune system to normally harmless substances—allergens—like pollen or food, and to irritants like cigarette smoke or colds. (See chapter 1, "What Is Allergy?") Unlike other allergic reactions, however, it takes place in the lungs and not in the nose (as with hay fever), the skin (as with hives), or other organs. Since asthma interferes with the breathing process, it's helpful to understand how normal breathing works.

During normal breathing we take in air through the nose or mouth. Air passes through the larynx (voice box), into the trachea (windpipe), through the bronchus, and into the two bronchi, one supplying each lung. Inside the lung, the bronchi divide into thousands of branches, or bronchioles, each with a cluster of microscopic air sacs called alveoli at the end. The whole system is much like an upside-down tree with a trunk, branches, and thousands of small twigs. In fact, it's occasionally called the "bronchial tree."

In the alveoli the real business of breathing takes place—the exchange of oxygen for waste material. Inhaled breath in the alveoli provides oxygen, which is necessary for the body to produce energy. The oxygen is taken up by tiny capillaries and pumped throughout the body in the bloodstream. Carbon diox-

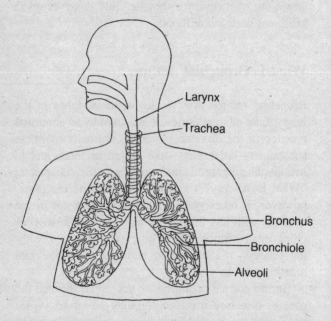

Figure 1. In normal breathing, air is taken in through the nose or mouth, past the larynx (voice box), through the trachea (windpipe), and into the bronchi, one leading to each lung. Air then passes through the smaller bronchioles and eventually through clusters of tiny air sacs called alveoli at the end of each bronchiole. The system is known as the "bronchial tree."

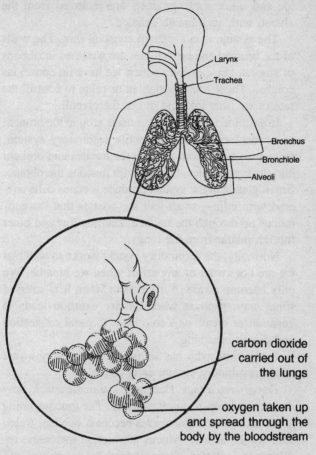

Larynx

Trachea

Bronchus

Bronchiole

Alveoli

carbon dioxide
carried out of
the lungs

oxygen taken up
and spread through the
body by the bloodstream

*Figure 2. The vital exchange of oxygen and carbon dioxide
that permits the body to produce energy takes place in the tiny
air sacs, the alveoli. As blood in the capillaries passes through
the alveoli, carbon dioxide is removed from the blood and
carried off during exhalation; oxygen from inhaled air is picked
up by the capillaries and pumped throughout the body by the
bloodstream.*

ide and other waste products are removed from the
alveoli with each breath exhaled.

The system is in a state of constant flux. The walls
of the bronchi and bronchioles are wrapped in ribbons
of smooth muscles over which we have no conscious
control. These muscles tighten or relax to control the
rate of air flow into and out of the alveoli.

In addition to the smooth muscle around the bronchi
and bronchiole walls, the entire respiratory system,
from nose and mouth through the trachea and bronchi
into the bronchioles, is lined with mucous membrane.
Small glands in the system produce mucous cells cov-
ered with cilia—small hairlike bristles that "sweep"
mucus up through the trachea, keeping dirt and other
foreign matter from the lungs.

Normally, the respiratory system works so well that
we are not aware of any effort when we breathe. We
only become aware of the system when it is stressed
some way, such as when intense exertion leads to
gasping for breath or a cold leads to nasal congestion
and mouth breathing.

But a child who has asthma becomes very aware
of his respiratory system early in life.

The asthma attack. During an asthmatic attack, several things happen simultaneously. The mucous lining
of the bronchi and bronchioles becomes swollen, which
narrows the airway. Mucus production increases, resulting in irritation, characterized by coughing, and
then obstruction, characterized by wheezing and shortness of breath. The condition is aggravated by bronchospasm, a tightening of the smooth muscles around
the airway. In severe attacks, the mucus actually plugs
up the air passages because more mucus is produced

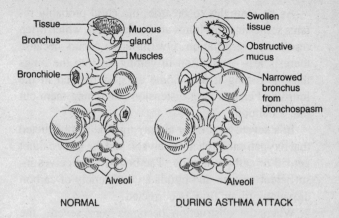

Tissue — Mucous gland — Muscles — Bronchus — Bronchiole — Alveoli

Swollen tissue — Obstructive mucus — Narrowed bronchus from bronchospasm — Alveoli

NORMAL   DURING ASTHMA ATTACK

Figure 3. In a schematic illustration of a normal bronchus (left) and a bronchus during an asthma attack, key changes can be seen. During an asthma attack, increased mucus production leads to obstruction of the bronchus and bronchiole; bronchospasm of the muscles wrapped around the bronchus narrows the airway; and the tissues in the bronchus swell, causing further congestion. Prompt treatment is often necessary to open the airway, release trapped air, and reestablish the carbon dioxide–oxygen exchange in the alveoli.

than the cilia can sweep out to keep the passages clean.

This narrowing of the respiratory system causes the violent symptoms of an asthma attack. The narrowed airways make it more difficult to breathe during exhalation than during inhalation because the bronchi and bronchioles are somewhat wider on inhalation. The child's increased efforts to exhale and, to a lesser extent, inhale result in the characteristic whistling sound or wheeze of asthma. The sound is caused by air forcibly exhaled through the narrowed tubes and the vibration of mucus.

As he struggles to breathe, the child probably retains some air in his lungs after exhalation, which often results in overinflation. Overinflation occurs because there is less obstruction in getting air into the lungs than in getting it out. Some air gets trapped in the lungs and causes lung distension, stretching them out like a balloon.

In a severe attack the airway may be so obstructed that oxygen can't reach the alveoli and the body cannot get rid of carbon dioxide. The body thus receives insufficient oxygen and builds an oversupply of carbon dioxide until air flow is corrected.

When the obstruction becomes very severe, the body's supply of oxygen starts to get depleted, and the carbon dioxide supply rises to a dangerous level. Carbon dioxide then combines with water and converts to carbonic acid; even more important, oxygen absorption is impaired. If the child is struggling for air and turning ashen, get emergency help *immediately* to avoid any serious consequences.

Infants having an asthma attack often react differently from older children. Instead of becoming frightened during an attack, an infant may experience shortness of breath, wheezing, and labored breathing, and still lie contented, even smiling and playing with crib toys. This docile acceptance makes the attack easier to bear, but as the infant becomes older and more active, he sheds the placid manner and becomes more anxious about the symptoms.

Why the asthma response. An asthma attack is caused by an allergen, the same mechanism that precipitates other allergic reactions. As explained in chapter 1, repeated exposure to allergens such as pollens, house dust, molds, animal dander, food, and so on, creates antibodies—blood proteins—in the immune systems of allergic people. After the antibodies have built up to a high enough level in the bloodstream, they start to react with the allergens upon subsequent exposure. When this occurs, powerful chemical mediators, including histamine, are released into the affected part of the body, provoking the symptoms of allergy.

The release of chemical mediators in the nose, eyes, and sinuses of someone with nasal allergy brings on sneezing, itchy eyes, congestion, and other nasal allergy symptoms. The release of mediators in the skin causes eczema, hives, and other rashes. The release of mediators in the gastrointestinal tract of a person with food allergy may cause diarrhea or vomiting.

In a similar manner, the release of mediators in an asthmatic child's lung tissue or respiratory airway walls causes bronchial obstruction, overproduction of mucus, wheezing, and other symptoms of asthma.

Warning signs of an asthma attack. In children, asthma attacks sometimes are preceded by a lingering cough that becomes worse with exercise (unlike the cough of nasal allergy), nasal congestion, runny nose, and a characteristic wheeze or whistling sound during breathing. Breathing in some cases is obviously difficult. Often an attack is also preceded by a respiratory infection such as a common cold.

However, other attacks may be surprisingly sudden with no warning and no obvious "trigger."

What Triggers Asthma?

Anything that can trigger allergy in one child can trigger allergic asthma in another—or in the same child. These things include a wide variety of allergens and many nonallergic irritants.

Allergens and asthma. The most common allergens in asthmatic children are inhalants or food.

Inhaled allergens include animal dander; grass, weed, and tree pollens; molds; and house dust. House dust and animal dander are usually more important as allergens during the colder months when your child spends more time inside. Pollen allergy is often seasonal—spring and fall. Animal allergies are not confined to dogs and cats; any hairy or feathered animal can cause allergic asthma. In general, that's any pet that doesn't crawl or swim. (See chapter 3, "Nasal Allergy," for more information about inhaled allergens.)

Food allergens that may trigger or worsen an asthma reaction are more common in children, particularly the very young, than in adults. Just how common is debatable, but in dealing with asthmatic children, allergists routinely explore the possibility of food reactions.

The most common foods or food families triggering asthma are dairy products, eggs, nuts, fish, and shellfish. Also fairly common are certain raw fruits (apples, melons, berries, citrus fruits) and vegetables (broccoli, cabbage, corn, cucumbers, green peppers, potatoes), spices, and wheat. Fruits and vegetables tend to be less allergenic when cooked than when eaten raw. Some allergists feel that food coloring is an important allergen, although this theory is controversial.

In infants, milk and eggs probably are most likely to trigger asthma problems if any food is at fault. Other prominent suspects are orange juice and wheat. (See chapter 5, "Food Allergy," for more information about food allergens.)

Multiple allergens are common in asthmatic children. If your child has asthma and is allergic to ragweed pollen and eggs, for example, he may get a reaction whenever he inhales the pollen or eats food made with eggs, but it *may* be necessary for your child to inhale the pollen *and* eat the eggs before an attack occurs. This is one of the reasons that allergens are often difficult to trace.

Nonallergens and asthma. Asthmatic children are generally more sensitive to nonallergenic irritants than children with other allergies, just as they are often sensitive to more different types of allergens than children who have a single other allergy.

One of the most common irritants—often the one that triggers the child's first asthma attack—is an upper respiratory infection (URI), such as a cold or flu. The infection stresses the lungs, making them more sensitive to allergens and less resistant to an attack.

Strong smells can often trigger an asthma attack, such as cooking odors, and any strong odor from paint, varnish, household cleaning supplies, or other harsh chemicals. Practically any pungent odor—the kind you notice on first opening the front door—can trigger bronchospasm (tightening of the muscles around the bronchi and bronchioles) in a child who is sensitive.

Temperature change also can trigger bronchospasm—a sudden change, such as rushing from a warm house into the winter chill. Temporary bronchospasm may not progress to a full-blown asthma attack, but must be treated as though it will. Sometimes it will subside as your child learns how to relax when she feels an attack coming on.

Sinusitis—inflammation of the sinuses—also can trigger an attack, as well as being a source of misery in itself.

Another common irritant, smoke, is theoretically easy to eliminate. Obviously it's best for your asthmatic child if no one smokes in the house. The difficulty of enforcing this rule depends on the number of smokers in your family and the tenacity of their habits. Guests and baby-sitters should be asked to refrain from smoking when the child is present. The irritant is not only tobacco smoke, but any smoke, including that from burning leaves or grass clippings.

Be sure your child's immunizations are kept up to date. Your asthmatic child should receive the same immunizations as any other child—for diphtheria, pertussis (whooping cough), and tetanus, referred to collectively as DPT.

Polio oral vaccine is safe for your child, as is measles live vaccine unless your child is receiving cortisone treatment. Rubella (German measles) and mumps vaccines can be administered safely, and influenza vaccine may be prescribed if an epidemic is forecast, but should *not* be given if your child is allergic to eggs or chicken.

One further potentially troublesome situation is called the "aspirin triad syndrome." While the syndrome is controversial—allergists do not agree on its existence—what is usually meant is a combination of asthma, aspirin intolerance, and sinusitis with polyps. Some patients cannot tolerate the yellow food dye tartrazine either. A child with asthma, aspirin intolerance, and sinusitis, may touch off an asthma attack if she takes aspirin or tartrazine. The controversy over this situation centers on whether this collection of problems is interconnected enough to be called a syndrome, or the separate problems of asthma, aspirin intolerance, and sinusitis really do not have that much to do with one another.

In any case, most allergists do recommend that allergic individuals, particularly those with asthma, avoid aspirin and use aspirin substitutes, such as Tylenol® or other brands of acetaminophen.

Exercise pros and cons. Good physical health promotes good mental health, for your asthmatic child as for any other. He's not as likely to feel unduly sorry for himself if he's participating in sports and games to the best of his ability. Taking part in a variety of activities with his peers will give your child a good attitude and a good self-image, and will prevent his disease from feeding a sense of alienation. (See chapter 8, "Raising an Allergic Child.")

Exercise can, however, trigger an attack of asthma. Most asthmatic children—some 60 to 70 percent—begin wheezing after five to six minutes of continuous, strenuous activity such as running. If your child has a slight wheeze to begin with, his reaction can be worse. This does not mean children with asthma cannot take part in athletic activities; it means they must be selective.

Sports that require short bursts of energy with rest periods in between, such as tennis or baseball, generally are much better tolerated by asthmatic children than is, for example, basketball or cross-country run-

ning. Your attitude can be a big help. Encourage him
to test his own limits. If his condition is not severe
(most asthmatic children are in this group), he should
find out for himself what he can do. He'll learn to
take prescribed medications before exercise if needed,
which activities are most comfortable for him, how to
time his rest periods, how to anticipate attacks, and
how to handle them with medications and relaxation.

One quirk of some asthmatic children is that they
may perform well on one day and poorly on the next,
for no discernible reason. If your child reacts this way,
he'll have to get used to some inconsistency. You can
help a great deal by your understanding. Encourage
him to enjoy his good days and accept the bad ones.
Don't be an overdemanding parent breathing down his
neck.

The emotional component. We've come a long way
from the days not long ago when asthma was considered an emotional disease. It is not. It is an allergic
reaction of the respiratory tract in sensitive individuals
to allergens or irritants.

Emotional stress can play an important role, however. It can trigger attacks in some children, although
it does not *cause* the asthma. It's important to recognize that emotional stress doesn't mean just anger,
anxiety, or fear. The stress can be intense excitement,
such as the frenzy of a crowd at a close football game,
or a series of belly laughs.

Just as emotions can affect asthma, so can asthma
affect emotions. You cannot ignore the emotional suffering, the battering of the self-esteem that some children with severe asthma experience after repeated
attacks.

A child with asthma would be less than human if

she did not become frightened during her first attacks when she feels as though she's suffocating. And chronic apprehension can build up. She may live in constant fear of another attack. She will tend to protect herself, to be less adventurous and rough-and-tumble than other children her age. In addition to wheezing a great deal, she may sniffle and snort from nasal allergy or get unsightly rashes from a skin allergy. It's small wonder that some children so afflicted feel different from their peers and left out.

This is where your support, along with proper medical treatment, can help tremendously. Such a child does not need overprotection. Your willingness to have her take part in all sorts of activity with her peers, to extend her limits, and to accept what she cannot change matter-of-factly, can be the kind of support she needs most. (See chapter 8, "Raising an Allergic Child," for a more detailed discussion of allergy and emotions.)

Diagnosis of Asthma

In an infant or child, the characteristic wheeze, cough, shortness of breath, and other telltale symptoms usually make it fairly easy for your doctor to diagnose probable asthma. However, those symptoms can also point to other conditions. A careful doctor pays attention to the aphorism "All that wheezes is not asthma," and considers other possibilities.

If the doctor sees your child in the emergency room during an early attack, she may quickly check to see if the child choked on something that could be caught in his windpipe. She may later check for bronchitis and for bronchiolitis. Bronchitis is an inflammation of the bronchial passages. (Asthma is sometimes called "bronchial asthma," but it is not the same thing as bronchitis.) Bronchiolitis, a viral infection of the smaller bronchioles, may mimic asthma in infants younger than six months. It usually is associated with an upper respiratory infection and often occurs in epidemics; it becomes "something that's going around."

Also, in the early stages of what appears to be asthma, your doctor probably will do a thorough physical examination and run laboratory tests to rule out other uncommon but potentially serious possibilities, such as cystic fibrosis and tuberculosis.

If the diagnosis of asthma is questionable, she may use other diagnostic techniques such as blood counts, further X-ray studies, determination of IgE levels in the blood serum, pulmonary function tests (measuring how well the lungs work), and so on. Skin tests often help pinpoint the allergic triggers; they are more helpful with inhaled substances and less so with food triggers. The radioallergosorbent test (RAST) serves much the same function by detecting specific antibodies. (See chapter 3, "Nasal Allergy," and Appendix B, "Radioallergosorbent Test [RAST].")

Keep in mind that nearly always, your physician can rule out other possibilities and can diagnose asthma and begin treatment on the basis of a thorough physical examination and a complete history. (Sophisticated testing is available, but it's seldom necessary.)

Treatment of Bronchial Asthma

Asthma in your child is reversible, which is the medical term for treatable. Unsettling as some asthma attacks are, they can almost invariably be managed with simple treatment and no resultant lung damage. Treatment can improve the quality of life for virtually all children who have asthma.

It's important, however, to guard against overtreatment. Treatment should be warranted by the symptoms; no new therapy should be prescribed unless your child requires it to lead a high quality of life. A child with a mild asthmatic condition who has a flotilla of medications is apt to become overly preoccupied with her asthma.

That said, it's well to know that there are three general approaches to treatment: avoiding the triggers, immunotherapy (allergy shots), and medication.

Avoiding the allergens and irritants. Obviously, this is the most effective treatment for any allergic condition, not just allergic bronchial asthma. Determine the source of the allergy and remove it or remove your child from it. Theoretically, this method is foolproof. Practically, it is nearly always impossible to do completely. Your child may well react to multiple allergens and irritants. Even when these are all known, you can't very easily remove all pollen, eliminate all dust or mold, and get rid of all fumes. And removing your child—moving to another city, another state— often results in his trading one allergen for another and is seldom recommended.

Still, there is much you *can* do. You can cut back

on house dust, fumes, and other household triggers if they are part of your child's problem. There's no need to convert your house into a hospital, but removing real dust collectors and cleaning your child's room (where he spends half of his time) regularly and thoroughly certainly will help. Air conditioning too can be a basic help, at least in your child's bedroom, in cutting down on airborne allergens. (See chapter 3, "Nasal Allergy.")

You'll have responsibilities aplenty if your child is affected by certain foods and needs diet changes. Even so, keep it as simple as possible. Eliminate a food from his diet only when you and your doctor are convinced that it's at fault, and try to substitute a nutritionally comparable food to keep your child's diet as balanced as you can. (See chapter 5, "Food Allergy.")

Immunotherapy. Also known as hyposensitization, desensitization, and most commonly as allergy shots, immunotherapy helps in some cases when other treatment fails. When your doctor identifies a specific allergen he will administer low but gradually increasing doses of it to your child every week. The goal is to achieve an increased tolerance when the child is again exposed to the allergen. (See chapter 3, "Nasal Allergy.")

Medications. For the great majority of children with bronchial asthma, occasional oral medications are all that's required for symptomatic relief.

But remember, you need careful control over any medications. Be sure you and your child follow your doctor's instructions on prescribed medicines. And with nonprescription drugs (dozens are available in drug stores and supermarkets), don't get in the habit of self-treatment. If your child has asthma, your doctor should be the one to determine what medications she receives, how often, and in what amounts, including nonprescription medications.

This carries a responsibility too. Your doctor should unfailingly explain possible side effects to you. If she does not do so with every medication prescribed for your child, *ask* what the important side effects are. If you don't understand her explanation, ask again. You really have no choice but to make certain you know what to watch for, even if your doctor does not volunteer the information. You see your child more than anyone else, so you will be the first to notice any signs of an adverse reaction to medication.

Categories of medications. Medications in the treatment of asthma fall into three basic categories—bronchodilators, preventive medicines, and steroids.

Bronchodilators, sometimes called bronchial dilators, are the most widely used medications for asthma in children. By relaxing the muscles surrounding the bronchi and bronchioles they help prevent asthma attacks from getting out of control. Theophylline, one of the most popular bronchodilators, is available as a pill, a liquid, or a capsule. It is also available as a suppository but most physicians oppose the use of rectal medicines in children. Adrenergic bronchodilators—a different type—are also available as a liquid, a tablet, shots (primarily Adrenalin®), or aerosol sprays.

"We strongly urge that bronchodilators such as theophylline preparations or adrenergic agents be used at the onset of the cough or even earlier, to *prevent an attack* from progressing," advises Warren Richards, M.D., head of the Division of Allergy and Clinical Immunology at the Children's Hospital of Los Angeles. "The longer you wait to treat an asthma attack, the less likely you are to control the wheezing."

The medication is usually taken with an aerosol inhaler or a nebulizer. Aerosol inhalers contain a liquid form of bronchodilator under pressure; nebulizers contain similar liquid medication but as a pumped spray. Both methods of inhalation first break the medicine into exceedingly fine particles.

One precaution: Be sure your child does not use an inhaler more often than your doctor prescribes. This is a real possibility because some children experience relief from using an inhaler and use it much more than they should. Overuse can result in severe side effects and can actually make the asthma much worse.

Bronchodilators usually are prescribed not only to contain an acute attack of asthma but also to prevent it. Once an acute attack is underway, the mainstay of therapy is an injection of epinephrine. It acts swiftly and nearly always provides full relief.

"Even with proper use, both bronchodilators and epinephrine have the possibility of adverse side effects," Dr. Richards says, "such as stomachache, headache, nausea or vomiting, shakiness, irritability, and wakefulness. They are usually not serious but talk them over with your doctor if they appear—especially if they cause your child to lose sleep."

In addition to bronchodilators, two recently developed medications are proving very effective in the prevention of asthma attacks—cromolyn sodium (Intal®) and beclomethasone (Beclovent®, Vanceril®).

"Both are to be taken when the child is well to help him stay well," Dr. Richards says. "They may irritate the airways, so it is extremely important that the child's chest be clear when the medications are given. In fact, it's very important to *stop* cromolyn sodium or beclomethasone when a child begins wheezing, and switch to another medication."

In children with frequent asthma attacks, cromolyn sodium often is prescribed first. Allergists believe it works by inhibiting the release of chemical mediators such as histamine from the mast cell, thus preventing the allergic reaction. It also appears to decrease the "twitchiness" of the lungs. Beclomethasone, on the other hand, appears to decrease inflammation.

Steroids also are used in treatment of asthma, primarily to lessen inflammation in relatively severe cases. They are prescribed for short periods of time (three to five days) in what doctors call "bursts." "Steroids are extremely potent," Dr. Richards says. "They do have a role in treatment and they do have side effects that must be watched. If your child needs steroids, your doctor will want to monitor their administration carefully. If steroids are used for less than a week, very few side effects occur."

What about expectorants? "There is very little evidence that shows the iodides or other prepared expectorants to be of benefit," Dr. Richards advises. "Iodides have significant side effects and many allergists are reluctant to prescribe them for children. The best expectorant is water. When a child has asthma attacks, it's very important that he drink a lot of fluids to counter any dehydration and to lessen the thickening of secretions in the bronchi."

So many drugs have been and are being developed

based on better understanding of the mechanisms of asthma that if one medication fails or produces too many side effects, your doctor nearly always can add or substitute another that will work.

Be sure that you, your child when he is old enough, and your doctor clearly understand what medications your child should take, both regularly and at special times, such as before exercising or at the beginning of an asthma attack. You need to know what medications, what dose, how often, and what common side effects to watch for. (See chapter 8 under "Your Child's Doctor.")

Further help with asthma. Under certain circumstances, your doctor may recommend postural drainage exercises and breathing exercises. The breathing exercises are chiefly for relaxation. The postural drainage exercises help your child remove mucus that may remain in her lungs and airway. Self-hypnosis and transcendental meditation also are sometimes used to promote relaxation.

Chances are very good that your child will not require either exercise, but if needed they can be helpful.

COMMONLY PRESCRIBED MEDICATIONS FOR ASTHMA IN CHILDREN*

I. BRONCHODILATORS

A. Theophylline

1. Short-acting

Tablets
Aminophylline

Liquids
Slo-Phyllin®
Accurbron®
Choledyl® Pediatric
Somophyllin®

2. Sustained Action
Slo-Phyllin® Gyro-
caps
Theo-Dur®
Somophyllin®-CRT

B. Adrenergic Agents

Liquids and Tablets

Metaprel®	Alupent®
Brethine®	Ventolin®
Bricanyl®	Proventil®

Sprays

Isuprel®	Medihaler®
Metaprel®	Alupent®
Bronkometer®	Ventolin®
Proventil®	

Injections
Adrenalin®
Sus-Phrine®
Terbutaline

II. PREVENTIVE SPRAYS

Cromolyn Sodium (Intal®)
Beclomethasone (Beclovent®/Vanceril®)

III. STEROIDS

Prednisone

*This chart does not constitute an endorsement of any medication but reflects the prescribing pattern of Warren Richards, M.D., Head, Division of Allergy and Clinical Immunology, Children's Hospital of Los Angeles.

5. Food Allergy

There's little doubt that allergy due to food is more common in infants and young children than in adults, but beyond that the subject is open to controversy. Some physicians feel that as many as 30 percent of allergies in infants and young children are caused by food, but most consider that figure much too high. Many allergists are convinced that food allergies are overdiagnosed—that some reactions are said to be from food when in fact they are due to other allergens.

Tracking down a food or a food group causing a child's allergy can be time-consuming and difficult. It takes dedication and insight by parents and doctors because an allergic reaction to food can occur in nearly any body tissue and can run the gamut of symptoms. Gastrointestinal symptoms such as stomach cramps and diarrhea are most common, followed by skin symptoms such as eczema and hives, and respiratory symptoms such as the sneezing and snorting of nasal allergy. Asthma can also be a reaction to food.

A certain food can trigger reactions in children ranging from very mild sniffling to life-threatening anaphylaxis. (See chapter 7, "Allergic Emergencies.") Infants may be born harboring a food allergy tendency that shows up later; it is extremely rare for infants to have an allergic reaction during the first few weeks of life. A few may acquire a food allergy while being breastfed.

Some allergists believe that a child may be allergic to a combination of two foods when eaten together but not to each food separately, or to a certain food only when accompanied by a seasonal nasal allergy, an upper respiratory infection, or fatigue and chilling. In severe cases, some children can react from just smelling the allergenic food.

Extreme reactions are rare, but certainly do happen. For example, a very few children have what is called "restaurant asthma," a reaction to metabisulfite, a chemical used in many restaurants to freshen lettuce. In a recent California case, a child had an extreme anaphylactic reaction after eating only watermelon and lettuce in a restaurant; fast and extensive emergency treatment in a hospital saved his life. Allergists traced his reaction to the metabisulfite used by the restaurant to freshen and preserve the lettuce. At this writing, allergists are attempting to have the freshener eliminated from use in restaurants.

Tracing and treating a food allergy can soon lose any cloak-and-dagger allure it may have had initially. It's plainly frustrating in many cases, but that's where you're needed most — to keep searching and keep your

child on a strict diet if necessary. Remember that nearly
all children with food allergies can be helped dramatically, once you figure out which foods are responsible. It's a worthwhile search.

How Foods Cause Allergies

Reaction to allergenic foods can be either immediate
(within minutes at the most) or delayed for twenty-
four hours or more.

In immediate food allergies, the reaction is a con-
sequence of the basic allergen-antibody encounter. A
susceptible child is exposed to certain foods. Her immune system produces IgE antibodies to react with
those particular foods. The IgE antibodies attach to
mast cells in the lining of the digestive or respiratory
tracts or the skin. When a child with this defense
system on guard eats the specific food again, the food
and the IgE antibodies react and mast cells release the
chemical mediators, including histamine, which provoke the symptoms. (See Appendix A, "The Allergic
Reaction.")

Symptoms can be very mild to severe, including
shock. Common symptoms, usually mild to moderate,
are stomach cramps and diarrhea, hives and itching,
and sometimes wheezing and nasal discharge. (To learn
more about possible symptoms, read the appropriate
sections of chapters 3, 4 and 6.)

In a delayed reaction, symptoms do not appear as
dramatically as in immediate reactions. (Allergists are
not as certain about the mechanisms of delayed food
allergy. Many feel that the reaction may occur during

the digestive process, rather than upon ingestion of the food, as the allergenic substance is broken down and utilized by the body.)

Any food can cause an allergic reaction. In infants and young children the most allergenic foods are cow's milk, eggs (especially egg whites, because of the albumin in them), and wheat. In toddlers and older children, common food allergens also include fish, shellfish, berries, legumes, corn, melons, and pork.

Food additives and preservatives have come in for wide publicity in recent years as potential causes or triggers for a wide variety of problems. Some children have allergic symptoms after eating foods that contain additives such as colorings and preservatives, but how widespread and serious a problem this is remains very controversial. While some allergy researchers make a case for many additives causing asthma and other allergies, most allergists are more conservative in their assessment of the problem. The best approach for now is caution but certainly no panic. If your child seems to react to some foods containing additives, work with your doctor to determine if the additive is at fault and what should be done.

Special Problems in Infants

The greatest incidence of food allergies is in children during the first few years of life. But whether infants are ever born with a full-fledged food allergy is highly controversial. The controversy raises an obvious question: Exposure and reexposure to an allergenic food are necessary before an infant can be sensitized (made allergic), so how can a newborn infant be allergic?

The answer: The fetus, which can begin producing antibodies at twenty-two weeks, is sensitized by allergens inhaled or eaten by the mother. An allergen—say in cow's milk—can enter the mother's bloodstream and cross the placenta to sensitize a susceptible fetus. Thus it is possible for an infant to be allergic to cow's milk on tasting it for the first time. So goes the controversial explanation. In any case, such reactions are extremely rare.

Preventive measures in infants. Your diet during pregnancy and breastfeeding can be important if your baby has a high risk of developing allergies—if you, your spouse, and especially if both of you have allergies. Remember, you do not pass down an allergy, but a *tendency* toward allergies. Your hay fever may well show up in your baby as an allergic reaction to eggs or as infantile asthma. Discuss your diet with your doctor; he will know best how to combine your great nutritional needs during this time with those of your baby.

Other measures can help prevent or postpone food allergy in your baby. Some experts argue that you cannot prevent food allergies in an allergy-prone child, while others say food allergies *can* be prevented. In any case, it's clear that you probably can at least *postpone* food allergies, which is a big advantage. An infant's digestive system is not fully mature and allows food allergens to be absorbed directly from the intestine into the bloodstream. By the time the child is a year or two old, this direct transfer is blocked by a fully functioning digestive system. During the all-important first year, consider these antiallergy measures if your baby is at risk:

• Breastfeed your baby, if possible, for as long as you can and try to avoid feeding him cow's milk until he's at least one year old. Although some controversy still exists about breastfeeding as a preventive to allergies, most allergists strongly favor it. They point out that a baby is at least five or six times more likely to get food allergy if he's bottlefed cow's milk than if he's nursed by his mother.

• Discuss with your doctor using milk substitutes if necessary. If you cannot breastfeed your child and he has gastrointestinal problems from cow's milk, the popular soybean formula may *not* be a good replacement, even though it works well with most infants. There is now evidence that goat's milk is not an adequate replacement for cow's milk either; their allergenic properties are very similar. Your doctor probably will advise against using mocha mix as a substitute. Although well tolerated by most infants, mocha mix lacks adequate nutrition for some infants.

• Sometimes milk allergy is expressed as a combination of symptoms called Heiner's syndrome. If your child has frequent bronchitis, ear infections, chronic runny nose, occasional gastrointestinal symptoms, some GI bleeding (small amounts of blood in the stool), she may have Heiner's syndrome. Check with your doctor if your child has several or all of these symptoms. The doctor may recommend immediate elimination of milk from your child's diet, and do challenge tests to confirm the diagnosis, rather than first doing laboratory tests, which are not very reliable in milk allergy. Heiner's syndrome is uncommon but not rare, and it is controversial. Some allergists don't consider the symptoms to make up a real syndrome; most do.

• Be very cautious as you introduce new foods. Follow your doctor's recommendations, which probably will call for introducing new foods no more often than once a week and just one at a time.

• Wait for your doctor's okay, usually at about one year, before introducing foods likely to be allergenic, such as citrus fruits, eggs, cow's milk, wheat, fish, and corn. If your child develops an identifiable allergy to a certain food, your doctor may have you eliminate it from his diet. Test his tolerance for related foods too. (See "Watching for 'Related Food' Allergies," later in this chapter.) If your child is allergic to oranges, for example, be suspicious of lemons, limes, tangerines, grapefruit, and other citrus fruits.

• Watch for any and all allergic symptoms. Even when caused just by food, symptoms are far ranging. When your baby has the cramps of colic, as most food-allergic babies do, or wheezing, eczema, hives, sniffling, watery eyes, diarrhea, nausea, vomiting—pass the information to your doctor. Not all colic is caused by allergy, nor is all nausea or diarrhea; most is not. But with an allergy-prone infant, it's best to make sure.

• Since food-allergic babies often are predisposed to other allergies as well, be sure your baby's playthings are nonallergenic, keep the dust level low in her room, and minimize contact between her and family pets.

NOTE: Diets should be followed only under your doctor's supervision. An imbalanced diet can do much more harm than the problem. In fact, allergists sometimes see children who have been put on horrendous diets by their parents for minor allergies. Cases of severe malnutrition in allergic children through improper "homemade" diets have been reported. Check with your doctor before changing your child's diet.

Common Problems in Older Children

If your child had a food allergy as an infant, he is likely to have some kind of food allergy as a child. Often, if treated for a food allergy, he does in effect "outgrow" it, only to become allergic to other foods or other allergens.

Diagnosing food allergy. In some mild cases of food allergy, the diagnosis is apparent. If, in the early summer, your child eats the season's first fresh strawberries and immediately breaks out with a few hives, it's not hard to guess what caused the reaction.

But often it's not that easy to diagnose a particular food allergy. The history is the most important diagnostic procedure. The doctor may want you to keep a diary of foods your child eats and any symptoms she has, either immediate or delayed. A food diary showing what your child eats on "good days" and "bad days" can help your doctor pinpoint the food allergen or allergens involved.

Your doctor will ask details about your child's diet, symptoms, other diseases, specific foods that seem implicated, what medications your child is taking, and so on. He will try to determine any seasonal variation too, such as hives and wheezing from eating corn on the cob, that happen only during a heavy ragweed pollen season. And he certainly will want to assess the severity of the reaction. Treatment depends not only on identifying the offending food, but also on considering the effect. Is it a mild eczema once or twice a year, or severe hives and breathing problems every time the food is even nibbled?

If your child has gastrointestinal problems, your doctor probably will consider several other possible causes the first time around before checking out food allergy. Bowel problems in children, for example, are a more common cause of stomach cramps than are allergic reactions to food.

Food intolerances, unlike food allergies, trigger a gastrointestinal reaction even though the mechanism is not an allergic response. Some children, as they grow older especially, become intolerant to the lactose (sugar) in milk. They lack the enzyme lactase in their intestines to metabolize (break down) lactose. The lactose then is eliminated as part of the stool; it pulls along with it a lot of liquid and causes diarrhea and cramps. Lactose intolerance sometimes is mistaken for milk allergy, but your doctor can differentiate by laboratory tests.

When your doctor diagnoses a probable food allergy, she may prescribe a dietary trial to be sure. She may ask you to remove the food from your child's diet for a week or two and then serve the child larger than usual amounts for two or three days. If the symptoms reappear, that particular food is almost surely at fault. Depending on the severity of the reaction and the importance of the food to the child's diet, you may be asked to remove the offending food permanently from his diet, or to minimize his exposure to it.

If diagnosis proves difficult, the doctor may conduct a dietary trial called a "challenge test." After eliminating the suspected food, you "challenge" the child with large quantities of it—more than you would normally give for a dietary trial. To verify milk allergy, for example, your doctor probably will have you eliminate all milk and milk-containing foods such as cheese and custard for a period of time. If your child improves, the doctor will challenge him with fairly large quantities of milk to see if the original reaction, which may have been just a subtle rash, reappears and gets worse. If so, your doctor may eliminate milk and milk-containing foods again for a period of weeks and challenge your child a second time. (Challenges are always done when your child's condition is stable, not when he's uncomfortable.) Most allergists do a challenge test three times before declaring a definite relationship between the symptoms and the food in question. They want to be sure a reaction is not coincidence.

If your child has symptoms often, even daily, the offending food probably is something eaten frequently and not ordinarily thought of as allergenic. Your doctor may order a special elimination diet—stop everything and substitute a diet of normally nonallergic foods. Then reintroduce other foods one at a time. This test is time consuming and detailed; it should be conducted by an allergist, not a pediatrician or family doctor. Fortunately, it is seldom necessary in children.

Other diagnostic procedures for food allergies, such as physical examination and laboratory tests, are the same as for other allergic conditions. Skin tests are seldom necessary in children and are seldom as helpful as they are in detecting airborne allergens. Food extracts suitable for use in a skin test are too difficult to obtain from many foods.

Some experts feel that skin testing for food allergy

may be reasonably effective, but many do not. RAST tests of blood serum, while seldom needed, generally are considered somewhat more reliable than skin tests. (See Appendix B, "Radioallergosorbent Test [RAST].")

Treatment of food allergy. In children, elimination of the offending food is the only effective treatment, although medications help control symptoms. Immunotherapy (allergy shots) is ineffective in children with food allergies.

Your child's diet, without question, is the key to good treatment for whatever allergic condition the food causes. Diet is within your control, with this limitation: Follow your doctor's recommendations but try not, as some parents do, to become a slave to the diet. Don't let the treatment get worse than the disease. Common sense is the key. For example, if your child gets a mild eczema after eating a chocolate bar, she probably is allergic to it, but not seriously. Your doctor may want chocolate eliminated from her diet. However, if your child's sixth birthday is coming up and she wants a chocolate birthday cake more than anything else, common sense (with your doctor's blessing) would say let her have one. See that she takes any medication she's supposed to, and let her enjoy the cake along with her party friends.

If your child reacts violently to chocolate—if a taste of chocolate keeps her up all night with asthma symptoms—she, of course, should have no chocolate in any form. The danger of a severe reaction often is the deciding factor. If the predicted reaction is more a bother than a danger, bending the diet at times can be the best thing you can do for your child's health and happiness.

(This example may be contributing to chocolate's "bad press." Many allergists feel that chocolate is not nearly as allergenic as it's made out to be.)

There are some allergy cookbooks on the market, which can be a help if your child is allergic to basic foods. A few are listed under "Suggested Sources of Further Information," and your doctor may be able to recommend others.

Watching for "Related Food" Allergies

If your child is quite allergic to a specific food, he also *may* be allergic to other items in that food family. Some food families are well known, such as related citrus fruits, but others are not. For example, if your child is allergic to peanuts, he's more likely to be also allergic to beans than to other nuts because peanuts are in the legume family with beans, while other nuts are in a variety of food families (not necessarily related to each other, much less to peanuts).

The following list includes food families commonly causing food allergies. If your child is highly allergic to one food within a family, be suspicious of other foods in the family, but do not eliminate them without your doctor's recommendation.

Family or Group	*Related Foods*
Amphibians	Frog's legs
Banana	Banana
Buckwheat	Buckwheat, kasha, rhubarb
Cashew	Cashew, mango, pistachio

Family or Group	*Related Foods*
Cereal	Barley, bran, corn, malt, millet, oats, rice, rye, wheat
Citrus fruits	Grapefruit, lemon, lime, orange, tangelo, tangerine
Composite	Artichoke, chicory, dandelion, endive, lettuce, sunflower seed
Fish	All freshwater and saltwater fish
Fowl	Chicken, duck, game hen, goose, pheasant, turkey
Fungi	Mushrooms, yeast (baker's and brewer's)
Ginger	Ginger, turmeric
Goosefoot	Beet, spinach, Swiss chard
Gourd	Cantaloupe, casaba, cucumber, honeydew, pumpkin, squash, watermelon
Grape	Grape, raisin
Heather	Blueberry, cranberry
Laurel	Avocado, bay leaves, cinnamon
Lily	Asparagus, chive, garlic, leek, onion
Madder	Coffee, cola
Meats	Beef, veal; lamb, mutton; pork; venison
Mint	Basil, mint, marjoram, oregano, peppermint, sage, spearmint, thyme (spices, extracts, and other non-herbal flavorings like poppyseed, nutmeg, vanilla, and black pepper are not in this family)

Family or Group	Related Foods
Morning glory	Sweet potato (called "yam" in the southern United States, but not the same thing as a true yam)
Mustard	Broccoli, Brussels sprouts, cabbage, cauliflower, horseradish, kale, kholrabi, mustard, radish, rutabaga, turnip, watercress
Myrtle	Allspice, clove, pimiento, paprika
Nightshade	Chili, eggplant, white potato, red and green pepper, tomato
Olive	Olive
Palm	Coconut, date
Parsley	Anise, caraway, carrot, celery, dill, parsley, parsnip
Pea (legume)	Black-eye pea, kidney bean, licorice, lima bean, lentil, navy bean, pea, peanut, soybean, string bean, wax bean
Pineapple	Pineapple
Rose	Almond, apple, apricot, blackberry, cherry, peach, pear, plum, prune, quince, raspberry, strawberry
Saxifrage	Gooseberry, red currant
Shellfish	Abalone, clam, crab, crayfish, lobster, oyster, scallop, shrimp
Stercullar	Chocolate, cocoa

Family or Group	*Related Foods*
Tea	Tea
Walnut	Butternut, hickory, pecan, walnut (chestnut, filbert, Brazil nut are each in separate families)

6. Skin Allergy

Allergic conditions of the skin are common in children. Some common skin allergies, like poison ivy rash, are acquired, not inherited, so even children without allergic tendencies can get them. While skin allergies usually are not serious in themselves, they invite infections (which *can* be serious), and the discomfort—primarily intense itching—can drive a child crazy, with skin that feels on fire and that she's not allowed to scratch.

The child is subject not only to infections through the damaged skin surface of an allergic skin reaction, but also to emotional problems if the condition should become chronic. As children approach puberty, appearance becomes increasingly important to them. The child who looks in the mirror every morning and sees scaly patches or pimplelike hives has an emotional burden to bear.

The common skin allergies in children are eczema (atopic dermatitis), hives (urticaria), and contact allergy (contact dermatitis), including poison ivy reactions.

Eczema (Atopic Dermatitis)

Eczema doesn't just involve itching; eczema *is* itching. Ask any child who has it. Eczema is not life-threatening, but it can be torture, and the inevitable scratching can leave a child open to bacterial and viral infections.

The formal name, "atopic dermatitis," means allergic eczema, and nearly all eczema in children is the result of allergens or irritants. (Occasionally eczema is nonallergenic—more often in adults.) It can happen to any one at any age, but eczema is most common by far in allergic children; some 90 percent of all cases appear between the second month of life and age five.

Your child's risk of contracting eczema depends on his likelihood of being allergic. Young children with allergic tendencies are highly susceptible to eczema.

Eczema seems to go hand in hand with other allergies. Many youngsters who have asthma or a nasal allergy also get occasional eczema. Often the eczema crops up when they're quite young, only to be replaced later on by another allergy.

What it is. Eczema is a skin inflammation, the result of a reaction to an allergen or irritant. It is a superficial, excoriated, or scratched, red rash, dry and rather scaly. In very young infants, it appears on the cheeks and scalp, and later on the wrists, bends of the elbows, and behind the knees. It is *not* commonly located in the diaper area; don't confuse it with diaper rash.

The seriousness and extent of the condition vary greatly. Eczema can flare up and cover large areas of the skin, subside to a few slightly reddened spots, and then flare up again.

Eczema, like other allergic conditions, is not contagious, even though the skin looks it. The condition appears first as an excruciating itch. The child scratches, and where she scratches, the rash appears.

The primary characteristic of eczema that makes it difficult to manage is the intense itching. It's nearly impossible to control a child's scratching once the itching begins.

Not only will a child's scratching turn up more rash, it will also cause swelling of the reddened skin, and moist or "weeping" sores. If it persists, eczema causes the skin to become thickened, cracked, darkened, and crusted. It's not a pretty sight and very uncomfortable for the child. The damaged skin is a fertile breeding place for serious bacterial or viral infections.

The condition sometimes is difficult to treat and it is futile to try to predict the outcome of a case. Most cases that begin during the first few weeks of life do disappear or lessen considerably within two or three years, some within a matter of weeks. Most cases in children who become eczematous at ages four, five, or older are resolved by puberty (although certain cases fade for several years and *reappear* at puberty). Some eczema, usually in children who first get it as young infants, does persist into adult life, but these are severe cases and quite uncommon.

Causes and triggers. The precise cause of eczema

is not fully understood, but allergists agree that allergic eczema in infants is commonly triggered by foods. (See chapter 5, "Food Allergy.") Why one allergic child reacts to eggs by breaking out with eczema and another reacts with asthma or nasal allergy is still not understood.

In general, irritants that might worsen a case of nasal allergy will also aggravate and sometimes trigger eczema. Extreme temperature changes and dry, cold air often intensify a case of eczema. A few children may have more severe cases in the summer months, but far more have severe symptoms during the winter.

Irritants such as strong soaps and detergents (including bubble bath preparations) may increase the intensity of existing eczema and sometimes trigger a flare-up. Do not use anything to cleanse or soothe your child's skin that dries it or seals out air. In particular, avoid strong, heavily scented soaps and petroleum jelly. Keep the skin moist and allow air to circulate to prevent flare-ups. Symptoms of eczema are far worse when the skin is dry and flaky.

Rough clothing can also irritate your child's sensitive skin. Encourage him to let you know which clothes are most comfortable. Try to avoid rough wools that chafe and synthetic materials that keep air out. Cotton is always a safe choice. When you do have to choose a synthetic fiber, look for a loosely woven fabric that will breathe a little. Your doctor or the nurse may have some helpful suggestions for finding practical, comfortable clothing while avoiding the synthetic materials so much in use for children's clothes these days. And keep your child's clothing loose, but not so baggy that it will chafe.

As with other allergies, strong emotions and fatigue can also trigger or intensify eczema. Obviously you can't—and wouldn't want to—prevent your child from ever having a strong emotion or getting tired, but it is important to see that he goes to bed comfortable and relaxed so he'll sleep well. If he goes to bed tense and spends the night scratching, he'll be tired and cranky the next day and the whole situation will get worse.

Complications. Infection is the most serious complication of eczema. The open, damaged skin provides a point of entry and a fertile breeding place for bacterial and viral infections. If your child is eczematous, keep her away from persons with colds, chicken pox, influenza, and other communicable infections.

Viral infections are probably the most serious; if your child has eczema and comes in contact with another child who has viral fever blisters (Herpes simplex), your child can get a very dangerous infection. The same is true with smallpox vaccination. Smallpox vaccine should never be administered to a child who has eczema or to members of her immediate family, because of the possibility of picking up eczema vaccinatum, a serious viral infection. Fortunately, the vaccine is no longer required routinely in the United States.

Bacterial infections can also cause trouble. The most common are "staph" (Staphylococcus) infections, such as impetigo, and "strep" (Streptococcus), such as "strep throat." Both types are common in children. Antibiotics are usually prescribed.

If your child has eczema and develops an infectious disease (either a skin disease or a systemic disease such as influenza), both conditions must be treated. Let your doctor know when signs of skin infections (often yellowish pus or "weeping" of the rash) or symptoms of systemic infectious disease appear. They call for prompt treatment.

If your child has eczema for several years and reaches puberty with it, the mental anguish can be a serious complication. She may be increasingly disturbed about her appearance at the very time when appearances are most important. What can you do?

Keep in close contact with your doctor; many cases of eczema clear up at this time, so make sure everything is being done to produce a cure. At the same time, don't harp on the subject constantly or encourage your child to feel sorry for herself. A child doesn't need self-pity piled on top of frustration or anger over her appearance. Instead, help her pursue her talents and interests—sports, music, dancing, painting, whatever—so she'll be active and involved in things she loves, and, most importantly, so she'll develop a sense of accomplishment that will go a long way to compensate for the insecurity she feels about her looks.

In all events, be available to your child. Don't overplay the eczema but don't ignore it; talk about it with her when *she* brings it up. Do everything you can to help her through a tough time with her self-esteem intact.

Diagnosing and treating eczema. Identifying a skin rash as eczema is not difficult unless it's complicated by a skin infection. The characteristic scaly red patches speak for themselves. But zeroing in on a precise allergen or irritant as the cause is more difficult—and not always worth the effort.

As he does with other allergic conditions, your doctor will ask for a detailed history when first seeing eczema in your child. It helps identify food allergens and occasionally inhaled allergens. Skin tests and elimination diets are often useful in pinpointing the causes.

If a food is determined to be the allergen, you may be asked to eliminate it from your child's diet. And if housedust, animal dander, or other inhaled allergens are implicated, your doctor will recommend cutting down your child's exposure to these substances along the lines described in the "Nasal Allergy" chapter. Since often the culpable allergens are never identified, however, the emphasis in treatment is the relief of the intense symptoms without aggravating them.

The most important thing is to avoid drying out the child's skin. Wash him in either the shower or the bathtub, but don't let him soak in the tub any longer than necessary to get clean. And don't use regular soap on eczematous skin as it often contains harsh deodorants or perfumes. Soaps recommended by many allergists are Lowila®, Dove®, Neutrogena®, and Basis® Soap. Your doctor may prescribe a nonalkaline cleanser or grease-free lotion such as Cetaphil® or Sebanil® instead of soap if your child's eczema is acute.

Ideally, of course, your child should not scratch. No scratch, no eczema. But there's no way that a child—or an adult—can resist scratching eczematous itching. Explain to your child the importance of not scratching, try to divert his attention when the scratching is fierce, and have him wear soft clothing with long arms and legs to help cut back the scratching a little. And even if all else fails, keep your child's fingernails cut short to decrease chances of infection from scratching with dirty fingernails.

But do *not* physically restrain your child to prevent scratching. If he's a baby, do *not* use "mittens" over his hands at night to reduce scratching. This is sometimes recommended but it shouldn't be. Babies will scratch anyway and can rub themselves raw with mittens, producing a burnlike abrasion that can be worse than the result of scratching. And physically restraining a child of any age to prevent scratching can have ugly psychological repercussions, making him feel "bad" (because he can't control his scratching) and trapped without lessening the torturous itching.

Medications are the key to relief of itching. Corticosteroid creams are probably the most important medication for eczema. Hydrocortisone cream or ointment ($\frac{1}{2}$ to 1 percent) usually can be applied to any part of the body, but you probably should not use stronger creams on your child's face. Be sure to check applications with your doctor.

Other anti-itching agents such as Atarax® or Vistaril®, or antihistamines such as Benadryl®, are often effective. And there are special topical ointments and lotions to help keep your child's skin moist. Your doctor may prescribe an ointment such as Eucerin® or lotions such as Alpha Keri®, Cetaphil®, or Lubriderm®. Be sure to follow the instructions; lotions and creams usually are applied as often as necessary to keep the skin soft and moist. Other skin medications such as Carmol® may help in some cases, but must not be applied to acute eczema when the skin is cracked and open because they will sting.

In extreme cases of eczema that do not respond to lotions and creams or to antihistamines, your doctor may have to prescribe an oral steroid such as prednisone for a short period of time.

Some anti-itching creams and lotions are available without a prescription, but don't take any chances— check with your doctor before you use one on your child. Improper treatment of eczema can be worse than no treatment; your doctor's recommendations will help you make sure your child is aided rather than hindered by medications.

Home remedies. What can you do when your child wakes up in the middle of the night with an itchy red rash and can't get back to sleep? If you have nothing that has been prescribed for such situations, call your doctor for advice. (If you cannot call your doctor at night or have trouble getting through to her at any time for legitimate questions, she may not be the best choice for the medical management of your allergic child. [See chapter 8, under "Your Child's Doctor."])

If you need to make do with something around the house, a home remedy that's always worth a try is a baking soda or oatmeal bath. Make sure that the water in the tub is lukewarm, not hot or cold. Add a cupful of baking soda or a cupful of oatmeal (regular or instant) or both, and slowly bathe your child using a soft washcloth. Pat her dry.

This soothing procedure sometimes lessens the itching, calms the child down, and lets everyone finish the night's sleep. If she's still tense and keyed up after the bath, a bedtime story and some warm cocoa or milk should help her relax.

Hives (Urticaria)

Hives (urticaria) are bothersome but seldom life-threatening. They are small swellings of the skin—pale welts surrounded by reddish inflammation (erythema)—that can be any size from pinpoint specks to three inches in diameter. They can appear anywhere on the body. They usually appear without warning, persist for a few hours to a day or two of itching, and disappear. Some cases become chronic or periodic, but rarely in children.

Angioedema, which may accompany hives, can be very serious and needs to be watched carefully. Whereas hives are swellings of the skin, angioedema is a giant swelling of deeper skin tissues. Hives may be an outward sign of angioedema underneath. Angioedema tends to produce swelling in hands, feet, lips, and tissues of the mouth and larynx. When swelling occurs in the laryngeal area, it can make breathing very difficult and should be treated immediately as a medical emergency. (See chapter 7, "Allergic Emergencies.") Swelling in stomach tissue can cause nausea, cramps, and vomiting; in head tissue it can cause headache similar to migraine.

Causes of hives. In many cases of hives, the exact cause is never known. There are often too many variables complicating the diagnosis. For example, hives may appear within an hour of the child's having eaten a full meal, romped in the snow, taken medicine for sniffles and fought with his brother. Which of these things triggered the hives? You'll probably never know. This is especially true of chronic hives that come and go for weeks and months. Hives may appear suddenly on any part of the body; they may disappear and recur at unpredictable intervals. Any food, any medication, nearly any allergy trigger can cause a case of hives. Common causative conditions in children are upper respiratory infection, food reaction, and seasonal airborne allergen reaction.

If your child is allergic and has nasal allergy or eczema or asthma, he may also occasionally get hives. Why some allergic children react to certain allergens with hives and other allergy-prone children do not get hives from the very same allergens is another phenomenon still to be explained.

Diagnosis and treatment. Your doctor will rely heavily on your child's medical history to diagnose hives and their cause. The hives themselves are fairly easy to identify but must be differentiated from skin eruptions that look similar, such as insect bites or scabies.

The hives often clear up by the time a diagnosis can be made. If they persist, which is not common in young children, your doctor may want to investigate your child's sensitivity to foods and medications. He may check your child's reaction to physical stimuli such as sudden changes of temperature, and surely will find out if any infectious conditions are present, such as parasites, hepatitis, or infectious mononucleosis. Even in persistent cases, a definite diagnosis is difficult. Your doctor may want you to keep a diary or see that your child does, relating symptoms to diet or exposure.

If persistent or periodic hives become a real problem, medications do help. The spectrum of medications is basically the same as for eczema. Anti-itching medicines such as Atarax®, Vistaril®, and Benadryl® are often used to relieve itching. If your child is bothered by sunlight, sunscreen lotions may be prescribed, and if she often gets hives after exposure to cold temperatures, Periactin® may help to prevent the reaction.

Keep in mind that hives are seldom a serious problem in children. They may appear and disappear without apparent cause and they do itch. Only when they persist or accompany angioedema is an intensive diagnostic search necessary, and this is the exception rather than the rule.

Contact Allergy (Contact Dermatitis)

Contact allergy is just that: an allergic skin reaction from something that comes in contact with the skin. Symptoms include swelling, reddened skin rash, and intense itching; the rash can appear anywhere on the body. Blisters often appear, break, and later form a crusty surface.

If this sounds like poison ivy, it's not just coincidence. Poison ivy is perhaps the most common cause of contact allergy in children. It is an acquired reaction and can happen to any child, allergic or not.

Poison ivy, oak, sumac. Poison ivy, poison oak, and to a lesser extent poison sumac cause contact allergy only when the child touches them, directly or indirectly. That is, if the child touches the leaves of the plant or touches his dog who just ran through the plants, he can get a poison ivy reaction. He will *not* get a reaction from a distance, but only when he makes contact with the resin, the sap that makes the leaves so shiny.

A reaction to poison ivy usually develops within twenty-four to forty-eight hours after contact and lasts for seven to ten days, sometimes a bit longer. The traditional "washing with a good strong soap" to prevent the rash from appearing is not recommended treatment. The strong soap will work no better than any other, and it's likely to irritate your child's already irritated skin. But an early washing of skin and clothes with a gentle soap *is* recommended to get rid of the resin.

Scratching can spread the rash only if the resin is still on the skin. After the resin has dried or has been washed away, scratching will not spread the rash. So, if you can persuade your child not to scratch during the first day or so after exposure, through some miracle of parenting, you may prevent the rash from spreading. But *don't* physically restrain the child to keep him from scratching, or bandage the area to "protect" it. Basically, you just have to let the rash take its course and interfere as little as possible.

Other contact triggers. Some substances, such as poison ivy or poison oak, can cause a reaction in anyone exposed, allergic or not. But in allergic children, nearly any substance can provoke a contact reaction—many plants, cosmetics (including powders and lotions), fabric dyes, soaps and detergents, paints, chemicals in rubber and metal products, and drugs and medications. Adults tend to come into contact more often than children with many of the possible triggers, such as nail polish, eye shadow, hair dyes, antiperspirants, and industrial chemicals. Children are more often affected by things like clothing or soaps.

Contact reactions from wearing sneakers with no socks, or from dyes in new clothing, do occur in some children, but this is uncommon. So is a contact rash resembling poison ivy where clothing has been in firm contact—the neckline of the collar, the waist, chest, and so on. The metal in zippers and metal clasps or buckles can produce the same sort of reaction, although this too is rare in children.

A common cause of contact dermatitis in allergic children, on the other hand, is bubble bath preparations. The use of either a bubble bath liquid or dishwashing liquid for bathing can cause severe itching of the skin and a very fine rash that looks much like "goose pimples." Allergic children who have dry and sensitive skin are especially bothered by this reaction.

Nearly any medication can produce childhood contact allergies when it is applied topically—in an ointment or lotion, for example. Common ones include penicillin, the sulfa drugs, streptomycin, and local anesthetics such as novocaine.

Diagnosis and treatment. Diagnosing a contact allergic reaction usually is not difficult; the rash lasting seven to ten days and the itching are characteristic in most cases. Identifying the cause also may present few problems if the child's history points to a likely substance. If your child played yesterday in the neighbor's yard where you now discover poison ivy and she now has what looks very much like a poison ivy rash, chances are good that she has poison ivy. As with any other skin allergy, some contact allergy triggers are obscure and may take a great deal of time and effort to track down. But it may become important to do so if your child has relapses, because the only really effective cure for contact allergy is avoidance of the allergen.

Beyond that basic treatment, medications are available to relieve the itching and decrease the scratching while the condition runs its course. Cortisone creams or sprays are often prescribed, as are wet dressings and starch baths. Antihistamines are used for itching. The specific medicine or other treatment depends a great deal on the stage of the rash: Is it just beginning; is it still red and dry; is it crusted and moist; is it becoming chronic? Your doctor will select the proper remedies for your child at the particular stage of the reaction.

In severe cases, which are not common in children, prednisone by mouth is sometimes necessary. If your child does take the steroid prednisone, be sure you follow your doctor's orders closely, as to both dose and duration.

7. Allergic Emergencies

Allergies and allergic asthma in children generally are mild or moderate and well managed by diet, avoidance of allergenic triggers, and medication. But there are times when a child with an allergic reaction needs to be treated by a doctor—and fast. Although these times are rare, it's essential to be able to recognize and respond to an allergic emergency. Here are the more common ones:

Uncontrolled Asthma Attack

If your child has asthma, the attacks are part of his life—and yours. They may be frequent or occasional, somewhat predictable or right out of nowhere.

The attack is often preceded by a cold or coldlike symptoms, itching, and coughing, but it doesn't have to be. The usual symptoms of an attack are wheezing and coughing. In a severe attack, however, the child

may also experience severe shortness of breath, choking, and a feeling of suffocation. An attack can be
highly stressful, but it usually responds to medications
and reassurance. Give your child the medicine your
doctor has prescribed for these situations.

*If you have given your child the medications to
control the attack and he obviously is not responding,
call your doctor.* If your doctor is unavailable, leave
word at his office and take your child to the nearest
hospital emergency room for proper treatment. Don't
feel awkward about it, don't hesitate to call your doctor, and don't delay getting to the ER.

*If your child does not respond to medication, if he
is pale and his lips are turning blue (due to cyanosis
from lack of oxygen), if he's delirious, agitated, and
drenched with sweat, and especially if his chest is
heaving and his neck muscles are straining, call the
rescue squad immediately.*

Even with an acute attack that does not respond
promptly to home remedies, chances are almost nil
that it will be life-threatening. But it can be a very
upsetting experience that leaves your child, and you,
dreading a repeat attack. The distress can be eased by
knowing that prompt medical help is available when
necessary. So if your child has asthma, speak to your
doctor about how to handle emergencies. He'll explain
what particularly to watch for in your child.

Anaphylactic Reactions

Anaphylaxis commonly means the most extreme form
of allergic reaction. It happens when mast cells abruptly

release chemical mediators that overwhelm the body's immune system and not just the invading allergens. No one is certain why some few children have anaphylactic reactions and others do not, although children who are allergic to several allergens may be more prone to it. When children with other allergies do have an anaphylactic reaction, it tends to be more severe. It can be triggered by anything that triggers an allergic reaction.

An anaphylactic reaction happens suddenly, sometimes within minutes after exposure. A child may break out in hives, develop nasal symptoms such as runny nose with severe itching, intense itching of the skin, reddened skin and eyes, and overpowering anxiety. This may be followed by breathing difficulty, especially in getting air into the lungs, and characterized by a whooping sound (a life-threatening situation) or severe wheezing and chest tightness. Also, vomiting, cramps, diarrhea, and convulsions can occur. In very severe cases, the child may go into shock and lose consciousness.

Your child may have some or most of these symptoms. An anaphylactic reaction is similar to other allergic reactions except that a severe anaphylactic reaction is sudden, much more dramatic, and overwhelming. If your child has one, *get her emergency medical help immediately*.

Anaphylactic drug reactions. One of the most common causes of anaphylactic reactions is the administration of therapeutic drugs. The reaction is faster after injection than after swallowing medication. For this reason, doctors ask if patients, especially children, have any allergies to medications before prescribing.

Penicillin and related medications such as ampicillin—among the most beneficial antibiotics—are also among the most common triggers of anaphylactic reactions in children.

When an anaphylactic reaction takes place in the doctor's office or hospital, your child has emergency care available. Many doctors prefer to start a course of antibiotics for an allergic child in their offices for this very reason.

If your child is beginning a course of antibiotics at home and has symptoms of an anaphylactic reaction, call your emergency number and get him to the nearest emergency room as quickly as possible. Time is of the essence, because he may need epinephrine injections, oxygen, intravenous feedings, or other anaphylaxis treatment. Epinephrine injections constitute the most important treatment.

Immunization reactions. Most doctors now recommend tetanus-diptheria booster shots every ten years, unless a tetanus booster is needed after an accident. Also, it's now recommended that children older than six *not* receive whooping cough vaccine, thus avoiding the danger of an adverse reaction.

Mild reactions to the bacterial vaccines (available against whooping cough, typhoid, paratyphoid, cholera, plague, and tuberculosis) and viral vaccines, such as flu vaccines, are common. Severe reactions to vaccines are rare. If they happen, they produce the typical symptoms of an anaphylactic reaction and the child needs prompt medical attention. Fortunately, she almost always is in the doctor's office for the vaccination and is treated promptly.

Anaphylactic food reactions. Certain foods, such

as seasonal fruit, eggs, wheat, fish, and corn, that trigger an allergic reaction in some children, also can trigger an anaphylactic reaction in a very few children. The exposure doesn't need to be strong, either. If your child is highly sensitive to, say, fish, eating just a bite of fish can produce a reaction, and in extreme cases, so can simply smelling the fish cooking.

Mild reactions to allergenic foods are fairly common, and simply mean you should remove the offending food from your child's diet if it can be surely identified. Severe anaphylactic reactions to allergenic food cause the classic symptoms, including labored breathing, intense itching and reddened skin, profuse sweating, and so on. *If you see the anaphylactic symptoms in your child, get him medical care immediately. Call your emergency number and get him to an emergency room.*

Your doctor will want to identify the offending food so it can be removed. This is the best long-term treatment; allergy shots are seldom effective in food allergies.

Anaphylactic reactions to administered allergens. Yes, once in a great while, allergens being used by a doctor to diagnose or treat allergies can produce anaphylactic reactions. It is a rare occurrence, and nearly always happens in the doctor's office where the patient is undergoing skin tests or allergy shots, so prompt corrective treatment is readily available. Allergists favor giving shots in their office for this reason, and do not recommend giving shots at home.

Your doctor may restrict skin tests if your child has had an anaphylactic reaction and use other means of identifying allergens. Allergy shots often remain necessary in spite of the child's anaphylactic tendency, but must be regulated according to other variables, like the length of time between doses, the pollen season, and so on. This is a precarious balance to strike, and should be left to your allergist.

Anaphylactic insect sting reactions. Most children will react to a bee sting with sharp pain, a small hot reddened area on the skin, a raised whitish bump, and a few hours of discomfort. That's a normal reaction.

Abnormal symptoms after a sting are the same as with any anaphylaxis and may include breaking out in hives, nasal congestion, severe nose and skin itching, reddened skin and eyes, overpowering anxiety, breathing difficulty (especially on inhaling), a whooping sound, severe wheezing, and chest tightness. Also, a child may have vomiting, cramps, diarrhea, convulsions, and, in very severe cases, shock and loss of consciousness. *If you see in your child the signs of anaphylactic reaction to an insect sting, call your emergency number and get emergency help as quickly as possible.*

Anaphylactic reactions to insect stings are not as common in children as they are in adults, because children haven't lived long enough to build up a lot of prior exposures. The reaction can be just as devastating when it does occur though.

Children are stung most frequently by honeybees, yellow jackets, wasps, and hornets. In addition to these insects, fire ants, found in the Southeastern United States, are a problem. They inflict a painful one-two— a sting and a bite—that can produce serious reactions in children allergic to insect stings.

Of these insects, only the honeybee leaves behind

its identification—its stinger is barbed and comes off with the venom sac as the bee flies off the skin. If your child is stung by a bee, carefully scrape the stinger and venom sac off with a fingernail or knifeblade. Don't crush the venom sac as you do this, or you will inject more venom into the wound.

Another type of reaction to insect stings is just swelling, which usually does not progress to an acute allergic reaction and does not require emergency treatment. Just ice packs or cold packs will help. The swelling usually begins some twenty-four hours after the sting.

To protect your child, rely on your common sense. If your child is allergic to insects, she should not work or play around the lawn or garden, should wear shoes at all times outside, should wear white or light clothing in summer, should not wear scented lotions. Remove insect hives from around your house when you find them either by yourself or with the help of an exterminator. Your hardware store or garden center may be able to offer insecticides and advice. Sweetened food or garbage is a strong attraction for these insects, so keep sweet spills wiped up and keep the garbage area clean.

If your child has allergic tendencies but has never had an anaphylactic reaction to an insect sting, she probably won't ever get one, but do watch her to be on the safe side if she gets stung. Remove the stinger if a honeybee did the dirty deed, apply ice or a cold pack to the sting to control swelling, and if you see any signs of an anaphylactic reaction, get her to the emergency room fast.

If your child has had an anaphylactic reaction to

insects, your doctor may supply you with an emergency insect sting treatment kit that includes antihistamines, possibly a syringe of epinephrine solution, and a Medihaler-Epi®, which provides epinephrine by inhalation. Allergists consider inhaled epinephrine only 10 percent as effective as an injection, but it may be enough to get your child to the emergency room safely. You may want to ask your doctor about the preloaded syringes containing epinephrine for persons with anaphylactic reactions to insect stings. Some are now on the market. They're simple to use; when you place the device against your skin, it shoots out a needle that injects the solution.

If your child is extremely allergic to insects such as bees or wasps, your doctor may also suggest allergy shots. The best allergy shot program in the world doesn't guarantee that your child will not react to a bee sting, but it does mean that the reaction probably will not be as intense. Immunotherapy results are better now that pure venoms are being made available. Pure venoms are used both to diagnose (through skin tests) and treat (with allergy shots) insect sting allergies.

In both uses, however, the venoms are potentially hazardous. They themselves can occasionally cause allergic reactions. Allergists reserve allergy shots for extreme circumstances, when it definitely has been demonstrated that a child had a full-blown anaphylactic reaction to the insect.

8. Raising an Allergic Child

Depending on the severity of your child's allergies, they may have virtually no effect on his day-to-day activities, or they may pervade nearly every aspect of his life. If the allergies are moderate to severe, chances are that they interfere at least some of the time with his enjoyment of things other children take for granted. Given the discomfort he feels, the special attention he receives, and the experiences he misses out on, it's tempting for him to start thinking of himself as "different" from other children. One of the most important things you can do for him is to prevent this self-pity from taking root. Your goal should be to encourage him to live life to the fullest, not to shield him from every sniffle or rash. There's a lot you can do to smooth the way for him physically and emotionally without coddling or overprotecting.

Your Child's Doctor

If your child is allergic, or you think she might be, your first responsibility is to see that she receives proper medical attention. If she does have an allergy she may need ongoing medical care for many years and it's important that she trust and respect her doctor. By seeing that your child is treated by the right doctor, and setting the tone for their relationship, you insure not only that your child will get appropriate medical treatment, but also that she will accept the discomfort and inconvenience of tests and medication with as good grace as possible. Ideally, the doctor is a source of information, support, and encouragement for both parent and child, someone you can turn to often for advice and reassurance. You should be able to count on him to answer your questions and assuage your fears clearly, courteously, and authoritatively.

Allergist or pediatrician? Most childhood allergies are well handled by family doctors or pediatricians, who bring in an allergist for consultation if necessary. So if you suspect that your child has an allergy, the first person who should examine him for it is his regular doctor—the one he sees for well-baby checkups, school and camp physicals, immunizations, and other routine care.

The great advantage of this arrangement is that the family doctor or pediatrician knows your child already. She knows what your child is like when he's healthy, so she is in a better position than any other doctor to tell what is "normal" and what is not for your child. You both have some idea of what to expect from her, and if you've continued seeing her for some time, presumably you are reasonably satisfied with the care you've been receiving. So, unless the child's allergies are too severe, too complicated, or too time-consuming for his regular doctor to handle, it's best to rely on her.

What if your child's allergies *are* severe or complicated? In this case, your pediatrician will usually refer you to a board-certified allergist. Board certification means that the physician has had formal and lengthy training in allergy in addition to his pediatric or internal medicine training and has met the requirements for certification by the American Board of Allergy and Immunology. Not all board-certified allergists are right for you, but they are well trained, have passed intensive testing, and are in the mainstream of allergy management. The allergist will have access to more sophisticated methods of diagnosis and treatment than most pediatricians.

If your pediatrician or family doctor does not refer you to an allergist, but you feel that your child is not responding to the treatment he's receiving, voice your doubts to the doctor. Simply tell her that you're a little worried and describe the symptoms you observe (for example, he's still missing a lot of school, he's often tired and cranky, he has to be excused from gym class a couple of times a week). Remember that you see the child every day, and the doctor does not. She can't be aware of this kind of pattern unless you speak up. After describing the pattern, ask her directly: What's going on? Why doesn't he seem to be getting better? Why is he missing so much school? Should he be seen by an allergist?

If your child shows no improvement over the weeks and months, or even becomes worse, you are justified in doubting your doctor's analysis of the situation. If you don't get convincing answers to your questions, and the doctor still refuses to refer you to an allergist, it's time to take matters into your own hands. Call your county medical society or the allergy department of the nearest medical school for the names of local board-certified allergists.

In short, give your child's regular doctor a chance to handle the allergies herself, if she feels that that's the best course. But don't accept your child's becoming incapacitated without seeing an allergist. In many cases, the allergist can turn things around and make life easier and more enjoyable for your child.

What to expect from the doctor. Theoretically, the doctor should explain to you in as much detail as you desire everything you need to know about your child's diagnosis and treatment. Unfortunately, doctors are very busy people, and sometimes even the best-intentioned of them may forget or neglect to explain something to you. If he doesn't volunteer it, be ready with an arsenal of questions like these:

What is the diagnosis? What symptoms lead you to this diagnosis? What's the prognosis? What kinds of treatment are available for this condition? What are the pros and cons of each? Why have you chosen this particular course of treatment for my child? Is there something else we can try if this doesn't work?

Once a particular medication has been prescribed, make sure you get the answers to these questions: What's the medicine for? What's the proper dosage and how often should my child receive it? How long should she take this medicine? Can she give it to herself, or should I administer it? Can and should the prescription be refilled? What are the side effects to watch out for?

If the medication may induce side effects (most do), make sure you understand what the most common side effects are, how to recognize them, and when to call the doctor if they appear. Your doctor will encourage you to be on the alert for the telltale symptoms; there's no point in creating a medication-induced condition that's worse than the allergies themselves.

Ask the doctor how he handles emergency calls. Your child needs twenty-four-hour-a-day, seven-day-a-week coverage for emergencies and emergency advice. The doctor will have some arrangement whereby he or another physician sharing his night and weekend calls will be able to speak to you or see you in an emergency, with the child's medical records available. Make sure you know the procedure, and what number to call. Keep that number by the telephone, and if you need it, don't hesitate to use it.

When you have a question or problem that is not an emergency, call during the doctor's office hours. Chances are that he won't be able to speak to you right away, but you should expect him to get back to you that day, or the next day at the latest. If you have trouble reaching him within a reasonable amount of time, let him know. It may be that others are having the same trouble, in which case the doctor should set up a call-in hour or develop some other system for handling calls more promptly.

Emotional problems and the doctor. As you know, allergies affect and are affected by emotions. (See

"Emotional Development" in this chapter.) If your child seems to be having emotional or behavioral problems, whether they seem to be connected with the allergy or not, talk them over with the primary care physician and, if you see one, the allergist. A good doctor treats the whole child, not just his allergies. Often the doctor will have sensible, practical advice for both you and, if he's old enough, your child. She knows enough about children to be able to tell you if a behavior problem is "just a stage" or really something to watch out for. And most physicians are willing to play a supportive role in your family's growing up.

If the child shows signs of being truly disturbed or unhappy, he should be seen by a mental health professional. Discuss the problem with your pediatrician and ask for a referral to a psychologist, psychiatrist, or social worker—whichever she feels is best in your situation. While you should expect the primary care physician to be interested in the child's mental development and well-being, it is beyond the scope of her responsibilities to deal with serious emotional problems.

When to change doctors. It's not necessary for you to actively *like* the doctor in order for him to give your child good care. But you and your child should feel reasonably comfortable with him. If you don't feel that your doctor is giving your family adequate care, it may be time to consider changing doctors.

Don't take this measure lightly, however. It's important that your child, who is growing and changing every day, be seen regularly over the years by the same doctor. Only by seeing the child regularly can the doctor get a sense of what is "normal" and what is "abnormal" for your individual child. One child's "normal" level of activity may be unusually lethargic for another child. One child's "normal" body temperature may be too high or too low for another. An asthmatic child's "normal" level of wheezing is not normal for a nonasthmatic child, and so on. So before making a change, make sure that the problem with your present doctor is not something you can control.

If you're not satisfied with your child's progress, or you feel that a certain course of treatment is doing more harm than good, tell the doctor what you're unhappy about. Doctors are not mind readers, and unless you bring it up, the doctor may not be aware of the alarming symptoms, much less your anxiety about them. As a parent, you have special knowledge of your child, which the doctor, for all his medical training, does not have. So don't allow yourself to be intimidated by the white coat; if you're concerned, you owe it to your child to speak up.

Few doctors will resent this kind of concern on your part. They should be able and willing to answer your questions. If you don't feel satisfied with your doctor's explanations, ask politely for a referral to a specialist, or a second opinion. Then see what the new doctor says; after seeing someone else, you may feel reassured about the soundness of your doctor's advice, or you may like the new doctor a lot better and decide that in the long run it would be best to make the switch.

If the problem is more an emotional one—you or your child or both just don't like the doctor—you have to evaluate how much your personal feelings about the doctor are interfering with the child's medical treatment. If you feel that the doctor never has time for you, or is habitually rude, or evades perfectly reasonable questions, or treats you like an idiot, you may find yourself doubting his medical advice and even disregarding it at times. The doctor obviously doesn't believe in you, so why should you believe in the doctor? If the situation has reached the point where you don't trust the doctor anymore, it's time to find another. Children are very quick to pick up on their parent's uneasiness and distrust, and you'll have an awfully hard time convincing your allergic child to take the prescribed medication if you don't believe in it yourself.

If you like the doctor but your child doesn't, ask the child what frightens her or makes her uncomfortable about the doctor. Sometimes it's just a question of an unfamiliar physical trait, like cold hands, scary instruments, or a loud voice. Sometimes a shy or nervous child may need a little bit more gentleness or patience than most. Whatever it is, speak to the doctor about it. In most cases, he will be able to adjust his manner to make the child feel more comfortable.

After you've spoken to the doctor about the problem and agreed on some kind of solution, don't expect your child to warm up to the doctor instantly. Give them both a little time to work out their new relationship. If, after several visits, the child is still afraid of or uneasy with the doctor, in spite of your best efforts to accommodate them to each other, you may feel that a change is in order. Your child will accept medication and other restrictions ordered by the doctor with much less resentment if she feels that the doctor likes her and is on her side.

Finding a new doctor. If you have not gotten a

referral from your present doctor, probably the best
way to find a new doctor is to ask other parents. If a
friend of yours is happy with his or her children's
doctor, particularly if the friend also has an allergic
child, by all means give this doctor a try.

If you can't get a personal recommendation for a
new doctor, check with your nearest hospital, medical
clinic, or social welfare office for the names and addresses of pediatricians or family doctors in your area.
If you need an allergist, call your county medical society or the allergy department of the nearest medical
school for the names of board-certified allergists.

Your Child's Environment

When you stop to consider how much time your child
spends at home and at school, it's obvious that helping
to keep both environments controlled will be a great
benefit to him.

Deallergizing your home. If your child has moderate to severe allergies, it's important to control his
home environment. Even if he has a mild allergy, some
control of house dust is a good idea.

Be careful not to overdo. Some parents become
trapped by their own enthusiasm; they make such a
production out of cleaning the house that they're in a
continual state of fatigue and irritability. Their children
would much rather endure a few more sniffles and
have relaxed, energetic parents than live in sanitized
tension. No matter how severe his allergies, no child
should be turned into a hothouse flower.

Today with many parents both working full-time

outside the home, carrying out elaborate house sani-
tizing measures often is out of the question, but most
allergists agree that this is not a negative development.
Do what cleaning and rearranging you need to, without
making a big fuss about it. Treat it as any other household chore, like walking the dog or mowing the lawn.
Don't feel that you must do the entire job at one time;
start with your child's bedroom and do a little at a
time.

Here are environmental control instructions from
the Division of Allergy of the Children's Hospital of
Los Angeles, reprinted with permission:

DUST CONTROL INSTRUCTIONS

These measures are recommended for adequate control
of dust at home. They are most important in your
child's bedroom, because this is where one-half of the
child's time is usually spent.

• Your child's room should be as clean and as dust-
free as possible.

—Dust all surfaces with a damp cloth daily
(shelves, ledges, toys).

—Damp-mop all hard floors weekly.

—Clean walls and ceilings as needed.

• The air should be as free from dust and pollen as
possible.

—Keep windows and doors shut as much as possible.

—Air conditioners, air filters, or electrostatic air
purifiers are beneficial, but not essential.

—Place three layers of cheesecloth over all forced
air vents.

• Enclose mattresses and box springs with zippered plastic covers or allergen-proof fabric covers (the latter are cooler in the summer). Bedding should be changed and mattress cover damp-sponged or laundered weekly.

• Pillows and blankets should be of a washable, synthetic material. Feather, kapok, and foam pillows should be eliminated.

• Stuffed toys are tremendous dust collectors and must not be kept in the bedroom. Those kept in other parts of the house must be washable. Toys stuffed with cotton or kapok should be replaced with nonallergenic ones.

• Rugs and carpets also collect dust. If possible, floors should be vinyl, tile, or wood. If rugs are essential, they should be synthetic and short-pile, and must be vacuumed twice weekly.

• Keep books, if necessary in the bedroom, only in an enclosed cabinet.

• Clean furnace area and air conditioner filters monthly.

• Remove stuffed furniture (which also collects dust) from the bedroom or cover it completely with plastic.

• Use only synthetic curtains (nylon, polyester, or plastic), and wash them monthly. Avoid drapes, shutters, and blinds.

The list seems formidable, but it isn't as much work as it seems. Most of the steps are one-time moves, and the cleaning takes just a few minutes a day, once you've got the routine down. Nearly always it can be confined to your child's bedroom. Don't try to do it all at once or all over one weekend, and if you're really pressed for time, keep in mind that *anything* you can do to cut down the dust level and keep it down will be of great help to your child.

MOLD CONTROL INSTRUCTIONS

Mold (or mildew, as the resultant condition is often called) is a type of plant, a fungus, whose seeds (or spores) travel through the air and can cause allergic reactions. It is most common in damp and humid environments, especially in areas of decaying vegetation (gardens, forests, compost heaps, plowed fields) and water damage (closets, attics, showers, bathrooms, basements, home foundations), and in air conditioners, humidifiers, and vaporizers. Mold is often found on wicker, on damp furniture, under rugs, or in walls and baseboards where water damage occurs.

To help control mold exposure:

• *Remove all superficial mold.* A solution of Spic and Span® and liquid chlorine bleach is very effective in removing superficial mold. The solution should be prepared only in a plastic container. It should not be prepared or stored in metal. The solution is caustic and should be handled only with rubber gloves. Add one cup (eight ounces) Spic and Span® to one gallon of tap water. When this is well mixed, add one cup (eight ounces) liquid chlorine bleach (Clorox® or Purex®). Using rubber gloves, scrub all moldy surfaces using a small scrub brush in corners and hard-to-reach areas. Let the area dry for one or two hours and scrub again, using the same solution. Wash down with clean water and let dry completely. This procedure should be repeated whenever mold is present.

• Eliminate wicker planters, baskets, and furniture.

• Remove all decaying vegetation from all areas surrounding the house.

• If there is mold under the house, it may be necessary to *spray* with Bordeaux mixture, which can be obtained from most plant nurseries or garden stores. It comes in five-pound bags which should be mixed with fifteen to twenty gallons of water.

POLLEN CONTROL INSTRUCTIONS

If your child is pollen-sensitive, he should not garden, rake leaves, or mow grass. In addition, it is best that your child not be present when these tasks are undertaken; he should be inside or away at school or visiting a friend when outside yard work is done.

Your doctor will probably provide you with specific instructions for your child and her environment, but the general suggestions above are good guidelines for helping almost all children who are allergic to dust, mold, or pollen.

One final recommendation on measures to take around the house: If a pet animal is an important cause of allergy in your child and the reaction is severe, it's best to keep the animal outside the house at all times. If the reaction is moderate or mild, you may have other options, but under no circumstances should you allow the animal in your child's bedroom. (See chapter 3, "Nasal Allergy.")

Travel Precautions

Travel with a child who has allergy or asthma doesn't have to be a hassle. Just take a few commonsense precautions and don't get bogged down in intricate planning. Your child probably will welcome a trip; the accommodations along the way—airplanes, air-conditioned motel and hotel rooms, obliging restaurants—may bring some relief rather than more problems. These guidelines can help smooth the way:

Car travel. Be sure the air filter is clean and the air-conditioning unit (highly recommended) in your car is working well.

• When practical, keep the windows closed and the air conditioner on.

• Be sure the inside of the car is clean before you start, so the air conditioner doesn't circulate dirt and dust.

• If possible, drive at night. It may be easier than daytime travel, with less traffic and lower air pollution.

• Above all, don't smoke in the car.

Air travel. Traveling by air has the big advantage of speed. You spend less time enroute, which may benefit both you and your child.

• If your child has ear problems with his allergy, check with your doctor about possible medications for the flight, because changes in air pressure may create a few difficulties.

• If your child has food allergies, you may want to call in advance. Most airlines provide special diets if given enough warning.

• If the air terminal is crowded, and your child is bothered by the smoke and dirt, check with the flight agent. You may be able to board early. Be sure you and your child have a seat well away from the smoking section on the aircraft. But don't interrupt your child's excitement in the terminal or on the plane unless there's a good reason; let him enjoy the trip.

In general. No matter how you travel, remember the following practical pointers:

• Take an adequate supply of your child's medications.

• Check with your doctor for regular or special medications, and get her recommendations on who to see if your child gets ill.

• See that your child avoids camping out during the height of the pollen allergy season.

• If your child has severe asthma attacks, avoid wilderness camping (at a great distance from medical help) at any season of the year.

• Trips to relatives or friends are to be encouraged, as long as the host family knows about your child's condition and is willing to do a few things to make her stay comfortable, such as keeping a pet dog outside, vacuuming the rugs, eliminating problem foods, avoiding dusty jobs or outings. If there are too many allergy-producing factors, such as having to sleep in the guest bedroom in a dusty remodeled attic, it may be sensible to stay in a motel, although this must be weighed against the disappointment to child and host in such an arrangement.

• Closer to home, visits to friends' homes should be encouraged, as well as having friends in to play with your child. Simple explanations to the adults, and to the friends if your child wants you to talk to them, are all that's necessary to insure that he doesn't receive allergenic substances such as chocolate cake at a birthday party if he's allergic to it.

• Staying overnight, particularly as part of a slumber party, is fine for your child provided the host family knows of her limitations. Be sure you don't let your child wind up in a dry attic with seven or eight other kids in feather sleeping bags, accompanied by the family dog and cat. Your child may not want to bother anyone if she feels congested during the night, and may not call you when she should. To see that she has a good time, take sensible precautions: Explain the condition to the parents, have your child take her own nonallergenic sleeping bag and pillow, and have her take her medicine before she goes and bring some with her to prevent attacks.

• If your child is reluctant to explain his allergy to friends or parents on visits, offer to do it for him, or suggest what to say. Children do not want to feel "different" and allergies can foster that stigma. Be frank and positive in explanations: Your child has an allergy so he has to avoid such-and-such. Nothing's likely to happen, but if it does, he takes this medicine. And your child or his host family should call you if there's a question. The same sort of information, in perhaps more detail, should be given to a baby-sitter

when you hire one for an evening. Let people know—
and let your child hear you say it—that he handles
the allergy well and doesn't *let* it become a big problem.

The Allergic Child in School

It's natural to want to protect an allergic child from
any sort of stress, but if this tendency leads you to
allow your child to stay home from school when she
really doesn't need to, you're not doing her any favors.
Nor should she be encouraged to stay out of school
or group activities when there's no physical reason for
it. It's tempting enough for allergic children to spend
their time feeling sorry for themselves without the
added motivation of oversolicitous parents.

Furthermore, a school building, for all its children
and activity, usually comes closer to offering a good
physical environment for an allergic child than a home
does. Schools generally have very little stuffed furniture, no stuffed animals, little carpeting, and daily
floor maintenance.

So keep your child attending school regularly whenever possible and participating in virtually everything
the nonallergic children do. At the same time, realize
that the time may come when your child has an allergic
reaction or an asthma attack at school. Be sure that
the school personnel know about her allergy or asthma
and are prepared to help her when necessary. Equally
important, make sure that they know when no special
treatment is required.

Allergic children are sometimes sent home from

school needlessly and made to feel like outcasts for no reason except lack of information. Many teachers, principals, coaches, and even school nurses know very little about allergies. It's up to you to see that your child is treated properly by explaining to all who have charge of your child during the school day whatever they need to know about your child's condition.

What to tell the school. At the beginning of the school year, arrange to speak to all your child's teachers, the nurse, the coach or gym teacher, and the appropriate representative of the principal's office. This doesn't have to be a big, solemn conference, just a chat on the phone. Explain the child's symptoms, the diagnosis, times when the condition may worsen, what medication the child is taking, and what allergens or irritants he should avoid (for example, dust from nap-time floor mats in nursery school or kindergarten, paint fumes in the art room, certain foods in the cafeteria).

If the child's condition is likely to restrict some of his activities (for example, if paint fumes cause severe problems, he will not be able to take part in all of the normal art class projects), suggest alternative activities or projects that will serve a similar function, yet neither disrupt the class nor trigger a reaction. If paint fumes are a problem, the allergic child could go outside to the playground where another class is playing during his art period, and draw or sketch the other children playing in accordance with the art teacher's instructions. It is important that the child not be left with nothing to do during a class period (hence he should be given a specific project, not told to "draw anything you want"). Whenever possible, he should work on his project in the same room as the rest of the class, or, if that isn't possible (as with the paint fumes), he should not be banished to an empty classroom but left with another class under another teacher's supervision.

If the child is taking medication, especially an antihistamine, he may be drowsy or irritable some mornings. Explain to the teachers the effects of the medication, and ask them to let you know if the side effects interfere with his attentiveness in class. If the medication affects the child's performance in school, ask the doctor to adjust the dosage or try another medication.

If the child may need medication to control an asthma attack or allergic reaction, try to arrange for the school nurse to have the medication on hand. Unfortunately, some school districts forbid the administration of any drugs by the school nurse, but do your best to bend the rules. Make sure the nurse knows how to contact you during school hours (if both you and your spouse work, give the nurse all your phone numbers for work and home, and explain how to call you out of a meeting if that's likely to be a problem), and how to reach the doctor.

Some children experience temporary hearing loss from their allergies. Explain to the teacher that this may happen, so that he or she doesn't assume that your child is simply inattentive. Keep track of school-administered hearing tests, which often turn up hearing impairment as the first clue to the existence of an allergic condition, especially nasal allergy.

If your child may have an anaphylactic reaction or a severe asthma attack, explain to the school personnel how to recognize these emergencies and get immediate help. Make sure they understand how to tell a true emergency from a milder reaction, so they don't make a big thing out of a nonemergency situation—or ignore a life-threatening one.

If your child has asthma, explain to his teachers how to handle the occasional attack. The teacher should allow him to stop activity and rest as he works his way through the episode. If the wheezing persists or the child becomes upset or frightened, the teacher should take him (not send him) to the school nurse. The nurse should administer medication, if this is permitted, and let him sit or lie down quietly until he feels ready to rejoin the class. If the attack does not calm down, however, the nurse should call you.

A child with nasal allergy may often have symptoms that mimic a cold. Make sure the teachers and nurse understand that a runny nose, sneezing, red eyes, and the like are "normal" in your child and not indicative of a cold or other contagious disease. The child should stay in school unless he has a fever (anything over 100°F) or an earache, or feels so sick from the allergy or his medication that he can't function in the classroom.

A child with hives or eczema will sometimes come to school with unsightly skin or develop a reaction while at school. Explain to his teacher that the reaction is not infectious and not serious. The best thing to do about skin reactions is to keep the child busy with normal classroom activities; the more occupied he is, the less he'll scratch.

Physical education. Some limits on physical activity may have to be imposed by your doctor if your child is quite allergic or asthmatic, but try to keep restrictions to a minimum. It's best for your child to participate in regular physical education programs up to her capacity. Her performance should help determine limits.

Here's one place where you may have to insist on your child's freedom to try. And get your doctor's help if you need it. The tendency for years, especially with asthmatic children, has been to protect and shield, whether they need it and want it or not. The fact is that nearly all asthmatic children, unless seriously afflicted, can participate in nearly all physical education and many sports programs.

Asthma or allergies do *not* leave your child less strong or quick or well-coordinated or competitive. She may perform beautifully in regular physical education classes and even some team sports. The emotional as well as physical satisfaction of participation in these activities can be very beneficial, so resist any premature efforts on the part of the school to place your child in a corrective physical education program. This happens almost routinely in some schools. Call on your doctor for backing if you need to; do not let the school system hold your child back needlessly.

Even if your child is asthmatic, she probably will not have trouble with most physical activity, including intense workouts in fairly short bursts. She *may* have trouble with sustained physical activity without rest, such as running laps, depending on the extent of her condition. Duration is much more often a problem than is intensity. An asthmatic child is far more likely to do well in the long jump than in running the mile.

She may find that she needs medication before a physical event, or she may need a break to relax and avert an attack, and she probably will have to give up some activities in favor of others. But no child can do them all. She'll learn to work around her condition. She should be allowed to push herself, asthma or no asthma, and extend her personal limits. The days of tight restrictions and coddling because a child is labeled allergic or asthmatic are past, although it will take some effort to convince a skeptical teacher or coach.

A message from the doctor. Your doctor will help you handle your child's school situation in a way that's best for your child, given his condition. In general, most physicians approve the goals set forth in the following two form letters. From the Division of Allergy, Children's Hospital of Los Angeles, Dr. Warren Richards and Dr. Joseph A. Church provide the following letters over their signatures. We reprint them here with permission and thanks; they present a forceful case for a commonsense approach:

INFORMATION FOR THE ALLERGIC CHILD'S TEACHER AND SCHOOL NURSE

_____ is under our care for the treatment of allergy. As manifestations of the allergy, he/she may be expected to exhibit "snorting," nose-blowing and coughing (symptoms resemble a cold, but are *not* a cold). *If* the child has asthma, he/she may wheeze slightly. Please also note that temperature may vary up to 100.4°F in a *normal* (allergic) child without infection. It is extremely important that you understand that the above-mentioned patient is NOT contagious when he/she exhibits these symp-

toms. EVERY EFFORT SHOULD BE MADE TO KEEP
THIS YOUNGSTER IN SCHOOL! Under certain circumstances, we would like our asthmatic patient
to receive medications noted below while in
school.

Concerning activities, we would like the above
patient to engage in as much activity as his/her
capacity will permit. If asthmatic, the child may
have to limit activity during those times when
he/she is wheezing. Our primary objective is to
encourage this youngster to engage in as much
normal activity as is possible. Do NOT place this
patient in corrective P.E. unless advised to do
so by us.

This child's diagnosis is_____

He/she is receiving the following for his/her
asthma, and we would like him/her to be able
to receive this medication while in school:____.

The other letter specifically addresses the problem
of early shuttling of a child into remedial physical
education programs.

To Whom It May Concern:

The above-named youngster is under our care
for asthma and is able to engage in customary
Physical Education activities. However, because
of asthma, the youngster may have difficulty
engaging in track or "running laps." We would,
therefore, urge that the youngster not be forced
to run and, if necessary, be exempted from this

activity, but *should be permitted to set his/her own pace in regular Physical Education.* We strongly feel that transferring this youngster to Corrective P.E. would be detrimental to his/her mental health.

If you feel a letter like one of these would help your child, suggest the idea to your doctor. He'll probably be happy to oblige.

Emotional Development

Raising an allergic child can be frustrating, worrisome, and plain hard work. Fortunately, in most cases, the extra physical care that your child requires—keeping the house dust-free, cooking special foods, making sure she takes the right medicines at the right times, and so on—falls easily into line, once the new procedures become routine. The problem that may concern you the most is not the physical well-being of your allergic child, but her mental well-being. The stereotypical image of the allergic child who whimpers and whines her way through life, developing a hypochondriacal obsession with her infirmities and using them to tyrannize others, is still with us. You may wonder at times how to give her the special care she requires without overprotecting her. Like all children, your allergic child must be given the freedom to experiment, take risks, make mistakes, extend her limits, even at the occasional expense of her physical comfort. She may be allergic, but emotionally she is absolutely normal, and the more normally you treat her, the healthier and happier she will be.

"It's all in his head." One of the stumbling blocks in the path of many allergic children and their families is the still widespread belief that allergies are "all in the head." This old wives' tale is senseless and cruel, but many people may still say it or think it about your child.

To be as charitable as possible to those who tell you that your child's allergies are "all in his head," chalk it up to ignorance. Consider what they may see. When your child has symptoms like those of a cold, you say it's not contagious. When he wheezes, you still want him to stay in school. When he breaks out in a rash, you simply remind him to avoid certain foods in the cafeteria. People who are ignorant about allergy and asthma may ask themselves, Is he *really* sick? If he were, you'd keep him home. You would protect him. You don't do that, so it must be all in his head. He must be emotionally unstable, which certainly doesn't reflect well on you and your spouse.

Unfortunately, too many people still think this way. What can you do about it? Say it loud and clear and often: Allergies and asthma are not emotional diseases. As recently as ten to twenty years ago, even students in some medical schools were taught that emotions can cause allergies. Today, the evidence is in and it just isn't so.

The task force on asthma and the other allergic diseases of the National Institute of Allergy and Infectious Diseases—comprised of leading physicians and researchers in the field—has said: "There is no convincing evidence—despite attempts to link emotional factors with asthma and allergic diseases—that psychological problems themselves actually cause either." The same report does point out that "emotional factors may worsen asthma and aggravate other allergic reactions in people already suffering from the disorders."

Children who are allergy-prone are no more likely to have underlying emotional problems than are children who are not allergy-prone. Of course, if your child suffers from a chronic allergic condition, his allergy can affect his emotions and his emotions can positively or negatively affect (but not cause) his allergy.

This interplay of emotions and symptoms is associated with many chronic illnesses, such as epilepsy, diabetes, and peptic ulcers, as well as with allergic conditions. In fact, as you probably know from your own experience, emotional factors such as stress or depression can make a perfectly healthy person feel physically unwell, and a minor illness like a cold that drags on forever can make you feel unusually irritable or blue. In short, emotions affect everyone's health and vice versa, although the mechanism of this relationship is not yet well understood. With an allergic child, the relationship is just a little more obvious, because his physical symptoms are more obvious.

Manipulation. One emotional complication of childhood allergies is that many children learn to use their allergic symptoms to manipulate their parents into giving them special attention or favors. For example, an asthmatic toddler who is denied something she wants might naturally decide to throw a temper tantrum. In the course of her tantrum, she gets so worked up that

she starts to wheeze badly. Instantly her stern parent
is all kindness and sympathy. It doesn't take the child
long to figure out that a few wheezes are all it takes
to get what she wants. If this pattern goes unchecked,
by the time the child is school-age she will be a first-
class brat. It's not that she's faking the asthma—at
least not at first; it's that the frustration she feels at
not getting her way triggers an attack, which results
in her getting what she wants, relieving the frustration.
It becomes progressively easier for her to turn her
asthma on and off.

The best way to prevent this kind of manipulation
from becoming a problem is to be rigorously consis-
tent about discipline. Let's say your five-year-old is
screaming and crying because you won't let her have
some cake before dinner, and in the midst of her tantrum she starts to have a full-fledged and scary-looking
asthma attack. What do you do? You can't ignore her
severe physical symptoms, so sit her in a chair, give
her medication if it's been prescribed, and let her work
her way out of the attack (if she's really wheezing,
she can't continue her tantrum at the same time; she'll
quiet down of her own accord). But do not give her
the cake and do not make a big fuss over her. In other
words, *don't reward your child for having the attacks*.
Stay with her while she's having the attack and give
her what help and support you can to get her through
it, but don't give in on the issue you were at odds
about before the attack; keep that problem totally separate from her physical discomfort. Above all, don't
let yourself feel for one second the tiniest pinprick of
guilt that you "caused" the attack by not letting her
have the cake. You didn't cause the attack; the asthma

caused it. You were absolutely right not to let your child have the cake—or not to let her stay up past bedtime or whatever reasonable discipline you've imposed on her.

What if you suspect that your child is already an expert manipulator? What if he threatens to have an attack—or actually has one—every time he doesn't get his way? First of all, don't panic. Every child goes through stages of trying to manipulate his parents, and for the allergic child, the temptation is often too much to resist. It doesn't mean that he's a horrible brat; he's just being a child. It doesn't mean that you've failed as a parent; it just means that you're taking the bait and you have to figure out how to avoid doing it in the future.

Second, examine how you actually behave when your child has an attack. If he has been manipulating you successfully, chances are that his ploys work because you allow yourself to feel unduly sorry for him and just a bit guilty. You may feel guilty for having "brought on" the attack (which, as pointed out above, is nonsense), or for having "given him" the allergy (which, even if he inherited an allergic tendency from you, you had no control over), or for not being able to protect him from the distress of these attacks (nobody expects you to, including him), or just some vague, generalized guilt about not being a good enough parent. Think over your feelings and your behavior carefully; try to pinpoint what makes you feel this unnecessary, counterproductive guilt and how you communicate it to your child. Once you've figured out what's going on in your head, your guilt feelings will often seem silly and cease to be a problem. If you need some support and reassurance, it might help you to talk to a counselor, clergyman, or therapist—but make sure your adviser knows something about the nature of childhood allergies. If you like and trust your child's pediatrician, she may be the best person to talk to.

Third, stop playing into your child's hand. Be firm. Your child is not going to die of asthma because you won't let him go on that camping trip or get a dog. Treat his symptoms, but don't soften in any way about the subject in dispute. If he simply threatens to have an attack, don't be afraid to tell him: "Cut it out. You can wheeze all you want, but you still have to do your homework." In short, make sure he gains nothing by having an asthma attack. It may take a little practice to develop this firm attitude if you're used to capitulating to him, but it's worth the effort. If he succeeds in manipulating you, he'll try it on his friends, his teachers, and just about everybody else. Before long he'll have alienated a lot of people, leaving him lonely and you more distraught than ever.

By the way, it's no accident that asthma is the allergy discussed in the examples above. Asthmatic children seem to be the most prone to this pattern of manipulation because their symptoms are instantaneous and sometimes terrifying. That's not to say that other allergic children don't sometimes succeed in manipulating their parents through their allergic symptoms. For example, if your child is prone to hives and she absolutely does not want to go on a family camping trip, she may quite conveniently get a bad case of itchy hives the night before the trip. It's not that she can sprout hives at will; it's just that her anxiety about the trip may trigger a case of hives. If you've insisted all along that she go on the trip, then she should go, hives or no hives; allergic conditions should never provide an excuse for being inconsistent about discipline, unless the child is seriously ill (if, in this case, she had angioedema along with the hives, for example). But, of course, you would bring along plenty of medication for the hives; the discomfort of allergy is real, and should always be treated.

Tension-fatigue syndrome. Some children with allergies or asthma seem to develop a certain collection of symptoms (a syndrome) called the "tension-fatigue syndrome." Some allergists feel that this syndrome is caused mainly by the interplay of emotions and the physical symptoms of allergy, and some feel that certain food allergies are also involved. Others, however, feel that the "syndrome" is no more than a common manifestation of the physical stress that accompanies allergy.

The symptoms cited by proponents of the syndrome are these: The child usually has allergic "shiners" (dark crescents under the eyes), is pale and anemic-looking but not actually anemic, has a stuffy nose, sweats profusely, and complains of headache, stomachache, and occasional leg and back pain. He tires easily and generally appears ill.

If your child develops the syndrome, he won't have all these complaints simultaneously. The syndrome may develop unobtrusively, a symptom at a time. At a certain point the condition perhaps is heightened by loss of sleep and appetite, which leaves him exhausted. His exhaustion will in turn worsen the next asthma attack or allergic reaction and so on.

Most children become listless when they have the syndrome, but occasionally they react by becoming agitated, even hyperactive. Why? Allergists are still not all agreed on this. Some feel that this hyperactivity associated with tension-fatigue syndrome can be caused by any allergy; others feel that it is caused by food intolerance (allegedly most often to milk) and intolerance to food additives or dyes.

Yellow food dye No. 5 (tartrazine), used as a yellow-orange coloring in many prepared foods such as cakes and frostings, has been singled out by some investigators as a prime offender. In fact, the Food and Drug Administration requires that tartrazine in foods and drugs be listed with a cautionary note stating that some people may be sensitive to it. The sensitivity is often linked to aspirin sensitivity, but the significance and prevalence of such intolerance is still debatable.

Many allergists are not convinced that the tension-fatigue syndrome can be traced that neatly to a certain food or food additive, so they hesitate to recommend special diets. You may hear of the "Feingold diet," created by pediatrician Dr. Ben Feingold after reporting in 1973 his observations of benefits from a diet free of acetylsalicylic acid (essentially aspirin), sodium salicylates (essentially salt), and artificial food colorings and flavorings. A special conference held by the National Institutes of Health in early 1982 considered the evidence for such diets and found insufficient evidence to date that they cure hyperactivity, although a small number of hyperactive children have been aided by the Feingold diet. The NIH and many allergists recommend extensive controlled studies to determine any connection between diet and hyperactivity. In one controlled study, one child in eight appeared to benefit. If this ratio holds under further testing, diet might be a factor in controlling hyperactivity in some children.

Many allergists believe that the tension-fatigue syndrome is a combination of long-term physical and emotional effects of an allergic condition. They suggest that foods and food additives may be a part of it, but a small part. Whatever you choose to believe, everyone agrees that a child with any combination of the above-named symptoms should be seen by a doctor for treatment.

Family dynamics. It's little short of amazing how a small child with allergies can disrupt a whole family. Some disruption is usually unavoidable, but it need not be destructive. At times it may be difficult to balance the needs of the allergic child with those of other family members, but it's important to remember that each of your children—and you and your spouse—is equally special and has equal claims on your time and attention.

What's good for the allergic child is also good for the family in the long run, since anything that helps her to function normally will normalize the family as well. But at the same time, certain measures are not apt to bring cries of joy from her brothers and sisters.

Because of her, they may feel, they can't have a pet (or worse, have to get rid of a long-time pet!). They have to keep her room clean. They can't do this and can't do that because of their dumb sister and her allergies.

Along with this resentment of the restrictions that

the sibling's allergy imposes on them, the nonallergic children may be jealous of the extra attention the allergic child receives because of her condition. If the child's allergies are quite severe, this jealousy can become a real problem because the allergic child does in fact need a lot of parental attention in order to keep the allergies under control. You can't make it up to the other kids by ignoring your allergic child's health problems.

Along with the resentment and jealousy, a nagging sense of guilt may plague your nonallergic children. They know it's "wrong" to resent and sometimes even hate their sibling, who can't help having allergies and probably suffers from them a lot more than they do. But they can't help feeling angry or jealous at times; self-sacrifice doesn't come naturally to a young child. The guilt, rather than relieving the anger, tends to fuel it. The child who believes that he is bad because he has "bad" feelings about his allergic sibling is going to resent that sibling all the more for making him feel bad. His reasoning may go something like this: "I'm bad because I hate my sister, but if I didn't have a sister I wouldn't hate her and so I wouldn't be bad. My sister makes me bad and I hate her for it." It's a vicious circle that's hard for the child to break without your help.

What can you do to prevent or alleviate these feelings? To start with, make as few major changes in the household as you can—just those judged necessary by your doctor. Try to avoid making everybody give up something for the sake of one child. For example, if your son can't have stuffed toys or carpeting in his bedroom, there's no reason why your daughter can't keep her stuffed animals, plush carpeting, and ruffled bedspread in her room. If your daughter can't eat flour or eggs, your son can still have a traditional birthday cake. If the allergic child cries that "it isn't fair," as he will at times, you just have to point out that no, it's not fair that he has allergies and other people don't, but he can't expect everybody in the world to give up things they like because he can't have them. The shoe will be on the other foot just as often—when the nonallergic children claim that "it isn't fair" for them to have to give up something for the allergic one. When a major change does have to be made, let the kids gripe a little; it helps them ventilate their resentment. In the long run they'll be more philosophical about the necessary changes than if you preach at them about brotherly love.

Try not to let the allergic child disrupt family plans. Sometimes that may mean going ahead with a trip, a picnic, or a birthday party, even though his condition is likely to be affected a little. Prepare for these occasions in advance by making sure he's well rested and properly medicated. Obviously you may occasionally have to cancel a long-awaited event because the allergic child is really suffering, just as you would cancel if one of your other children were sick, but in general, it's best if the allergic child participates in as many family activities as possible. Don't court disaster, however. If you decide to visit your sister who has five cats, even though one of your children is allergic to them, the allergic child may have a reaction that will make him the center of attention for the whole visit. That kind of focusing on the allergies is exactly what you *don't* want.

When in fact it is true, explain changes in household routine as having been ordered by the doctor, rather than as something you or the allergic child wants. It's a mistake to make the doctor the fall guy for everything, because all your children should have a good relationship with him, but sometimes the siblings will accept a ruling from him better than they will from you. Talk to him about it.

Try to treat all the children fairly. "Fair" does not mean treating them all exactly the same. It does not mean that if Mary can't eat fruit, Johnny can't either. Each child is an individual with special emotional as well as physical needs. The allergic child may require a different kind of care, but she should not receive more care, more attention, more love than her siblings. She should never be seen as more needy or more vulnerable or less responsible and self-reliant than her brothers and sisters. She should share in chores and follow the same rules as the others. If she can't mow the lawn, she should do the dishes instead. If her eczema acts up, that doesn't mean she gets to watch an extra hour of TV.

Sometimes one of the children will have to give up something that's very important to her because of the allergic child. The obvious example is a beloved pet. If your daughter's cat must be given away because your son is allergic to it, make sure you tell her that you understand the sacrifice she's making and appreciate it. When she's ready, give her something or do something with her that's really special and just for her. Don't pretend that this treat, whatever it is, makes up for the loss of her cat. It's just a gesture of appreciation, a way of thanking and comforting her. By the same token, if the allergic child has to forgo something wonderful that the other children are doing, try to arrange some special treat for him as a substitute.

Finally, don't forget yourself or your spouse. Raising an allergic child should not become a full-time job. No matter how sick the child is, you need and deserve some time to yourself, and you and your spouse need time alone together. The most important people in a child's life are his parents, and unless they are happy and fulfilled, they can't give him the quality of love and care he needs.

When you feel frustrated. Some parents of allergic children feel that they have no right to be frustrated or angry. After all, parents are supposed to be wise, reasonable, compassionate, and *always* in control, aren't they? And how can you take out your own feelings on an innocent child? It's not his fault that he's cranky and irritable from his hay fever, is it? And it's not other people's fault that they don't understand about allergies.

Expecting yourself to be the perfect parent at all times is inhuman. When your child is whining nonstop because he's uncomfortable—when your next-door neighbor insists that the kid would outgrow his asthma if you'd just stop pampering him—when your mother-in-law accuses you of child abuse because you let him play baseball when he's obviously too delicate—you won't be the first parent to blow your top. An occasional outburst is nothing to be ashamed of. You're not a saint; some days it doesn't take very long to reach the end of your rope. Children need to learn that adults, even parents, are not always rational or in control. Sometimes they lose their tempers just like children. If you've really given your child a harder time than you meant to, apologize to him when you've calmed down, and then forget about it. He will too. As for those well-meaning outsiders, your little outburst may convince them like nothing else to keep their mouths shut in the future.

When things are not going well, it helps a lot to have an understanding listener to talk things over with. Someone outside the family whom you trust completely, someone who will listen to your doubts and complaints without criticizing or patronizing you, can often help you keep your perspective through some of the rough moments.

Above all, trust yourselves as parents. You love your children as no one else does, and you know them better than anyone else. Other people can help you, but ultimately you decide what's best for your family.

Children demand a great deal of their parents, and allergic children demand even a little bit more. But they don't demand that you be perfect. Don't demand it of yourselves.

Appendix A:
The Allergic Reaction

Depending on what part of the body is affected by the allergen-antibody encounter, an allergic child may have various reactions to allergens or triggers (rash, runny nose, hives, etc.), but no matter what the symptoms, the mechanism of the reaction is essentially the same. Research has led to a better understanding of the allergic reaction than we had just a decade or two ago.

Of the four types of allergic reactions, this book is concerned almost entirely with Type I—the anaphylactic-hypersensitivity reaction, or immediate hypersensitivity. This is the reaction that most of us think of when we hear the word *allergy*. It's the reaction of nasal allergy, most asthma and hives, most food reactions, and anaphylactic reactions. Reactions begin within minutes after the child is exposed to the allergen, and are *mediated* (set in motion) by the antibody immunoglobulin E (IgE). One of the five major an-

tibodies, or immunoglobulins, IgE is the major cause
of classic allergy symptoms, such as the sniffles of
hay fever or the rashes of contact allergies.

In allergic children, allergies begin with exposure
to antigens—plant pollens, molds, dusts, animal dan-
ders, some drugs, and other substances—that are
harmless to nonallergic people. An *antigen* that causes
an allergic reaction is called an *allergen*.

The child's immune system—the body's defense
system against unwanted "foreign" invaders such as
allergens and microbes—reacts to this first exposure
to the allergens by producing IgE antibodies. This
reaction does not produce any symptoms; it is the
body's way of getting prepared to defend itself against
the next allergen invasion.

Antibodies are specific. That is, each IgE antibody
will only react against the single allergen that it was
produced to counteract. An IgE antibody against ragweed pollen will react against proteins from a grain
of ragweed pollen, but not against tree or grass pollen.

These IgE antibodies attach to the surface of *mast
cells* or *basophils*. Mast cells and basophil cells are
very similar, although mast cells are found primarily
in the respiratory and gastrointestinal tracts and the
skin, and basophils are in the blood.

The next time an allergen enters the body, the IgE
antibody that has been produced to combat that specific allergen reacts with it to kick off the release of
potent chemicals from the mast cell or basophil. These
chemical mediators (chemical substances that activate
other parts of the immune system), especially a very
potent chemical called histamine, cause the symptoms
of allergy—the wheezing, sneezing, tearing, itching,

stomach cramps, diarrhea, and so on. The exact role of all chemical mediators has not yet been discovered, but researchers have determined that histamine causes itching and constriction of smooth muscle in the bronchial tubes, and increases the leakiness of blood vessels, which leads to swelling of tissues.

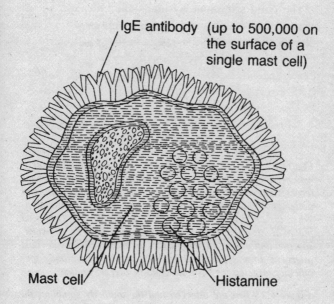

IgE antibody (up to 500,000 on the surface of a single mast cell)

Mast cell

Histamine

Figure A. The first step in the development of an allergy in an allergic child is exposure to an allergen. The child's immune system reacts to that specific allergen by producing an IgE antibody that can cause allergic reactions upon reexposure to that allergen. IgE antibodies attach in great numbers to the surface of mast cells (located primarily in tissues) or basophils (located in the blood).

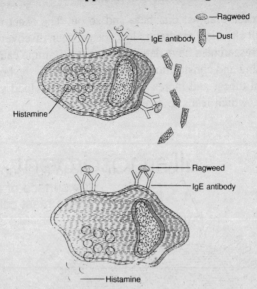

Figure B. Each IgE antibody reacts only with the allergens it was produced to counteract. An IgE antibody made to counteract ragweed pollen reacts only with another grain of ragweed pollen, not with dust, as shown in the schematic illustration. When the child is reexposed to the specific allergen (ragweed pollen in this illustration), the allergen binds with the ragweed-specific antibodies on the surface of mast cells, while dust allergens do not. Dust will be countered by an antibody specifically targeted for it, if the child is allergic to dust.

Figure C. When the allergen and the antibody combine, the mast cells release chemical mediators, including histamine. Histamine and, to a lesser extent, other chemical mediators cause the various symptoms of allergy, such as wheezing, sneezing, tearing, itching, stomach cramps, and diarrhea. The mechanism is a logical protection against invasion of the body by foreign and potentially harmful substances, such as bacteria. The problem with it is that in an allergic person the antibodies react against substances that are in no way harmful to a non-allergic person, overwhelming the immune system and setting off the galaxy of symptoms known as allergy.

Appendix B: Radioallergosorbent Test (RAST)

A recently devised blood serum test, the radioallergosorbent test (RAST) is in some use but is not totally perfected. Results, when interpreted by qualified physicians, can be an aid to diagnosis of allergies in some cases, usually in food allergies, but must be considered along with other information, especially skin test results.

RAST is an in vitro (test tube) laboratory blood serum test for allergen-specific IgE antibodies. It has been described as "a skin test in a test tube." The test measures the amount of specific antibodies in the serum—for example, the amount of ragweed IgE antibodies.

Most allergists agree that RAST gives as much information, when properly done, as a skin test. If a diagnosis is difficult, if the allergen being tested is potent or presents the possibility of an anaphylactic reaction during skin testing, or if a child should not receive skin testing due to eczema or other chronic skin conditions, a RAST may be ordered.

Generally, RAST is appreciably more expensive than skin testing for the same allergens, and not all laboratories are equipped to perform the test. When the test has been better standardized, so results from different laboratories are comparable, the RAST may be used more often.

Suggested Sources of Further Information

General Books on Allergy

Frazier, Claude A., M.D. *Parents' Guide to Allergy in Children*. Grosset & Dunlap, 1978.

Giannini, A. V., M.D.; Schultz, N. D., M.D.; Chang, T. T., M.D.; and Wong, D. C. *The Best Guide to Allergy*. Appleton-Century-Crofts, 1981.

Hirschfeld, Herman, M.D. *Understanding Your Allergy*. Arco Publishing, 1979.

Kempe, C. Henry, M.D.; Silver, Henry K., M.D.; and O'Brien, Donough, M.D. *Current Pediatric Diagnosis and Treatment*. Lange Medical Publications, 1980 (textbook).

Rapp, Doris J., M.D., *Allergies and Your Child*. Holt, Rinehart and Winston, 1972.

Young, Patrick, *Asthma and Allergies*. (Based on the

157

report of the task force on asthma and other allergic diseases, National Institute of Allergy and Infectious Diseases.) NIH Publication 80-388, 1980. (For sale by Superintendent of Documents, U.S. Government Printing Office, Washington, D.C. 20402.) Highly recommended.

Allergy Cookbooks

Emerling, Carol G., and Jonckers, Eugene O. *The Allergy Cookbook*. Foreword by Joseph F. Kelley, M.D. Barnes & Noble, 1975.

Nonken, Pamela P., and Hirsch, S. Roger, M.D. *The Allergy Cookbook and Food-Buying Guide*. Warner Books, 1982.

Other Sources of Information

A variety of information is available from the Asthma and Allergy Foundation of America, 9604 Wisconsin Avenue, Bethesda, Maryland 20814. The foundation can provide more than a dozen specific brochures (*Hay Fever*, *Food Allergy*, etc.), an allergy encyclopedia, a list of clinics and hospitals for asthmatic and allergic patients, audiovisual material on many asthma-allergy topics, and more for a charge. You may want to become a member of the foundation and receive its semiannual newsletter.

For additional information, write to the Office of Research Reporting and Public Response, National Institute of Allergy and Infectious Diseases, National

Institutes of Health, Building 31, 9000 Rockfield Pike, Bethesda, Maryland 20205.

The allergy and immunology department of your nearest teaching hospital or medical school may also be able to direct you to information.

Glossary

ALLERGEN. An antigen that can cause an allergic reaction in an allergic person. Plant pollens, fungi spores, house dust, and animal dander are common allergens.

ALLERGIC REACTION. An adverse response by the immune system of an allergic person to substances that are normally harmless, such as pollens and molds.

ALLERGIC RHINITIS. A nasal allergy, causing inflammation of the mucous membranes of the nose. Seasonal allergic rhinitis is commonly known as hay fever. See NASAL ALLERGY.

ALLERGY. An altered immune response in allergic persons to a specific allergen such as ragweed pollen.

ALLERGY SHOTS. See IMMUNOTHERAPY.

ALVEOLI. Tiny air sacs in the lungs, where oxygen enters the bloodstream and carbon dioxide is removed from it.

ANAPHYLAXIS. A severe, immediate allergic reaction that calls for emergency treatment.

ANGIOEDEMA. An allergic reaction marked by swelling of the deep layers of the skin.

ANTIBODY. A protein produced by the body to fight foreign materials that enter it; also known as immunoglobulin. An overproduction of antibodies stimulates the allergic reaction.

ANTIGEN. A substance foreign to the human body that provokes an immune response. See ALLERGEN.

ANTIHISTAMINE. The most widely used drug in the treatment of allergies. Dries up nasal tissues by blocking the action of the body chemical histamine, thereby interrupting the allergic reaction.

ASTHMA (ALLERGIC). An allergic bronchial condition characterized by some degree of bronchial airway narrowing, often accompanied by wheezing and shortness of breath; the condition usually flares up periodically in the form of asthma attacks.

ATOPIC DERMATITIS. See ECZEMA.

AUDITORY TUBES. Tubes connecting ear and throat, sometimes blocked as a result of allergy or infectious disease. Also called Eustachian tubes.

BASOPHIL. A type of white blood cell very similar to mast cells. See MAST CELLS.

BRONCHI. Airway tubes connecting the windpipe to each lung; they transport air into and out of the lungs.

BRONCHIAL ASTHMA. See ASTHMA.

BRONCHIOLITIS. Inflammation of the bronchioles.

BRONCHIOLES. Tiny airways forming a treelike network from the bronchi throughout the lungs.

BRONCHITIS. Inflammation or infection of the bronchial tubes.

BRONCHODILATOR. A medication that helps relax bronchospasm; often used to treat acute asthma.

BRONCHOSPASM. Tightening of muscles encasing the bronchial tubes.

CORTICOSTEROIDS (STEROIDS). Hormones produced by the body's adrenal glands; manmade corticosteroids are potent antiinflammatory medications. They are sometimes used to treat asthma and other allergies, but always with great caution.

DANDER. Small bits of animal skin, a frequent source of allergy (dander, rather than hair, is the primary allergen from pets).

DESENSITIZATION. See IMMUNOTHERAPY.

ECZEMA. An allergic inflammation of the skin characterized by intense itching. Also called atopic dermatitis.

ELIMINATION DIET. A diagnostic process to determine which food or foods are responsible for a food allergy; should be supervised by a physician.

EOSINOPHIL. A type of white blood cell sometimes collectively called "allergy cells" because it increases in number in the blood of allergic people.

EPINEPHRINE. The major treatment for anaphylactic allergic reactions and severe asthma attacks.

EUSTACHIAN TUBES. See AUDITORY TUBES.

FOOD ALLERGY. An allergic reaction caused by food, often characterized by stomach cramps, diarrhea, vomiting, rash, shortness of breath, etc.

GASTROINTESTINAL (GI) TRACT. The stomach and intestines.

HAY FEVER. See NASAL ALLERGY.

HISTAMINE. A body chemical released by mast cells during an allergic reaction, causing swelling, itching, and bronchial spasms.

HYPERSENSITIVITY. In a person previously exposed to an allergen, the condition that leads to an allergic reaction on further exposure; usually refers to nasal allergy and asthma.

HYPOSENSITIZATION. See IMMUNOTHERAPY.

IMMUNOGLOBULIN E (IgE). Antibody normally present in very low levels in humans but in higher levels during an infection and in allergic people. Thought to be the only antibody responsible for classic allergic symptoms. Other immunoglobulins studied are IgA, IgD, IgG, and IgM.

IMMUNOTHERAPY. Treatment of allergy by injection of identified allergens in gradually increasing doses; also called desensitization, hyposensitization, and allergy shots.

MAST CELLS. Cells in the mucous membranes, bronchial tubes, and skin that contain chemicals responsible for allergy symptoms. When allergens attach to IgE antibodies on the mast cell surfaces, the cells release chemical mediators of allergy.

MEDIATORS. Chemicals, primarily histamine, that activate other parts of the immune system.

MOLD. A fungus, such as mildew, whose spores can cause allergy.

MUCOUS MEMBRANES. Thin linings of the mouth, nose, and the rest of the respiratory system, kept moist by mucus.

NASAL ALLERGY. Allergy of the mucous membranes of the nose and mouth, caused primarily by airborne allergens. Also called allergic rhinitis. Seasonal (as opposed to perennial) nasal allergy is often called hay fever, sometimes rose fever.

POLLEN. Minute spores of flowering plants, a major source of seasonal nasal allergy (hay fever).

RADIOALLERGOSORBENT TEST (RAST). A test measuring the amount of certain IgE antibodies in a patient's blood serum as an aid in identifying causative allergens.

RHINITIS. Inflamed mucous membranes of the nose; can result from a nasal allergy (allergic rhinitis). Nonallergic rhinitis is usually caused by infection, hormonal changes, or certain drugs.

SEROUS OTITIS MEDIA. Inflammation of the middle ear, occurring mainly in children with nasal allergy; symptoms may be mild or absent.

SINUSITIS. Inflammation of the nasal sinuses.

SKIN TESTS. Dilute allergens are injected between skin layers (intradermally) or scratched onto the skin; if a reaction occurs, the tested allergen may be causing allergic reactions in the patient, but other evidence must be weighed before coming to a firm diagnosis.

STEROIDS. See CORTICOSTEROIDS.

TARTRAZINE. A yellow food coloring dye (U.S. Yellow No. 5) that may cause asthma or hives in some allergic patients.

URTICARIA. Hives. Surface skin swellings or welts of various sizes, usually red and itchy, most often caused by food allergies. Surface swellings sometimes signify angioedema.

Index

About the Author

Richard F. Graber, a free-lance medical writer and novelist, is a former senior writer and senior editor of *Modern Medicine*, *Geriatrics*, and *Patient Care* magazines. He lives in Connecticut.